Country Home®

AN OLD-FASHIONED

CHRISTMAS

Meredith® Books

Des Moines

COUNTRY HOME® MAGAZINE
Editor in Chief: Jean LemMon
Executive Editor: Ann Omvig Maine
Art Director: Peggy A. Fisher

Senior Editor: Beverly Hawkins
Copy Chief/Production Editor: Angela K. Renkoski
Interior Design Director: Candace Ord Manroe
Interior Designer: Joseph Boehm
Building Editor: Steve Cooper
Food and Tabletop Editor: Lisa Kingsley
Antiques and Garden Editor: Linda Joan Smith
Assistant Art Directors: Sue Mattes, Shelley Caldwell
Administrative Assistant: Becky A. Brame
Art Business Clerk: Jacalyn M. Mason
Editorial Trainee: Lisa C. Jones

Publisher: Terry McIntyre

MEREDITH® MAGAZINES
President, Magazine Group: William T. Kerr

MEREDITH® BOOKS
President, Book Group: Joseph J. Ward
Vice President/Editorial Director: Elizabeth P. Rice

AN OLD-FASHIONED CHRISTMAS
Editor: Jean LemMon
Project Editor: Marsha Jahns
Graphic Designers: Mary Schlueter Bendgen, Harijs Priekulis
Contributing Editor: Rosemary Rennicke
Contributing Writers: Candace Ord Manroe, Molly Culbertson,
Beverly Hawkins, Bob Brenner

All of us at Meredith® Books are dedicated to providing you
with the information and ideas you need for your home. We
guarantee your satisfaction with this book for as long as
you own it. We welcome your comments or suggestions. Write
us at: Meredith Books, Editorial Department, LS-348, 1716
Locust St., Des Moines, IA 50336.

The magic of Christmas is in its memories. And memories are very personal. Maybe to you an old-fashioned Christmas is candles on the tree and strap-on skates. Or maybe it's bubble lights and an electric train set. Whether the doll under your tree was a bisque doll, a Shirley Temple look-alike, or Barbie, those childhood Christmases create the memories we carry with us forever.

But no matter what our early Christmases actually were, there's another world of Christmas memories that we've taken as our own—one we've pieced together from books, drawings, old cards, antique toys, feather trees, and ornaments. This is the old-fashioned Christmas we may be too young to have lived, but we long for.

This is the Christmas of simple pleasures, of cherished traditions, of warm gatherings with family and friends. It is the Christmas you'll find on the pages of this book. And with this book comes my wish for you: May every Christmas, old-fashioned or otherwise, be filled with magic.

Jean Lem Mon

HOME FOR CHRISTMAS

Important every day of the year, the home has even more meaning at Christmas, when how we live says how we love. In their best holiday attire, each of the following homes warms from the hearth and the heart.

7

STARRY NIGHT AT STONEY FIELDS

It's a scene straight from the past: Sleigh bells jingling as horses pull the Brothers family, bundled beneath red-checked blankets, over the Vermont countryside. It's Christmas, as all of us wish it could be.

Like the first starlit Christmas long ago, the heavens twinkle with ancient light during December in Vermont at Stoney Fields—the hillside home of the Brothers family. Over the snow-covered hill the crisp night air rings with laughter and carols, and a family huddles close to a bonfire, sipping mulled cider from thermoses, in between songs.

"It's a Christmas Eve tradition," says Mary Brothers, who shares in the outdoor celebration with her husband, Richard, and their blended family of five children, plus grandchildren.

Right: Built in the classic New England style, the Vermont home of Mary and Richard Brothers is graced with snow-kissed garlands of greenery for Christmas.

Opposite: A balsam garland trimmed in berries and pinecones adorns the custom-made curving staircase in the entry hall.

"Everyone gets bundled up, and we build a big bonfire at the top of our hill and all go sledding," says Mary.

Afterwards, the family returns to the house—a 12-year-old classic New England-style home in Waitsfield, Vermont, that was built by Richard's contracting firm. Here, the family settles in for some bubbling fondue, stew, or chili—"something simple and hot that I've made ahead," says Mary.

"It's a wonderful way for us to spend Christmas Eve together, and we all look forward to it," adds Richard.

Heading indoors after such invigorating fun in the snowy night isn't at all anticlimactic, either.

STARRY NIGHT AT STONEY FIELDS

The celebration simply changes location. The home is every bit as seasonally appropriate a backdrop as the great white fields outside.

"It's a magical, enchanting season," says Mary, a decorator (she has had a shop in town for 20 years) who proves her talents in her own home at Christmas. "I don't like things to look contrived," she says. "Festive but natural is my goal."

Green wreaths, simple but elegant, hang both indoors and out. Garlands of evergreen boughs laced with gold beads spill over mantels and also down the bannister of the curved stairway, which is further made festive with large plaid bows and huge pinecones. Each window outdoors is adorned similarly, with natural garlands and cheery bows.

"The fireplace mantel is filled with greens, candles, cones, and gold beads," says Mary. "Green-and-red plaid bows, the smell of balsam, red and white poinsettias, and my traditional brandied apple cake are some of the sights and aromas that fill the house."

The large Christmas tree, commanding a prime space in the living room, is given much decorating

Left: *Formal dentil molding, a handmade Oriental rug, and a camelback sofa are softened in the living room with a mix of more rustic antiques, comfortable upholstered pieces, and holiday decorations, including natural wreaths and garlands and edible ornaments.*

Below: *Each year, the family gets together to decorate and hang on the Christmas tree as ornaments batches of cookies made in advance by Mary Brothers.*

STARRY NIGHT AT STONEY FIELDS

Right: *The blended family of Mary and Richard Brothers includes, left to right, back row: Lyle Johnson, Mary, Muriel Eaton (Mary's mother), Neil Johnson, Sarah and Anne Brothers, and Anne's infant son, Carter Lash. Seated in front are: Richard, John Wilson (Sarah's fiance), and Jim Lash (Anne's husband). Not shown is Mary's youngest son, John, who was away on a school trip.*

Below: *A balsam garland and gold beads decorate the mantel.*

attention, beginning long before Christmas Eve. Ornaments aren't saved, year to year, and hung on the tree. They're made anew each season: Every ornament is edible.

"Our family makes and decorates all the cookies that hang on the tree," says Mary.

Early in December Mary bakes batches of cookies and pierces each one with a straw, for hanging on the tree. Then she assembles frostings, decorating tips, and edible sprinkles and other decorations. At an appointed time, all of the children gather for a cookie decorating party—an ornament making party, in effect.

"It's fun for all of us to sit down together after everyone's been off doing their own thing," says Mary. "We have such a good time that it's become a family tradition. Some years, the children's friends have joined the group. They clown around and sing 'Frosty the Snowman' while they work on the cookies, and I have the best time listening to them."

The home itself, even without its special Christmas decorations, is conducive to drawing family and friends together. The interior design is what Mary calls "country formal." She explains: "It's certainly not rustic, but I do like living with country antiques."

Opposite: *An old bracket was added for architectural interest at the entry, blending with a walnut Victorian sideboard that belonged to Mary's grandfather.*

STARRY NIGHT AT STONEY FIELDS

Mary is drawn to furniture with a cottage feel, which means primarily transitional pieces caught somewhere in between precise design styles and periods. No one style is dominant in the Brothers' home, but pieces can range anywhere from Sheraton to Empire and on to Victorian.

"In the past, different woods were often used in the same room together, which is something I like to do," says Mary of her eclectic style.

For example, a country pine piece shares space with a dressier Victorian walnut sideboard in the hallway. And on a single furnishing, there's a blend of woods—a cherry chest with walnut knobs. Similarly, Oriental rugs warm the floors in some rooms, simple braided rugs in others.

"It all seems to blend together," says Mary.

Although credit for the comfortable sophistication and spontaneous mix of the interiors goes to Mary, the easy flow and efficient function of the spaces falls under Richard's bailiwick as a builder.

About five years ago, with their children grown and out of the house, the couple reexamined their life-styles and decided it was time for a change. The formal dinner parties of the past had given way to last-minute get-togethers, and the hub of the home had shifted from the dining room to the kitchen. It was time to remodel, enlarging the kitchen by actually relocating it to what was formerly a separate family room.

Now, not only is the kitchen itself much larger, but there's a built-in banquette area between the dining room and kitchen that is ideal for meeting the couple's needs. Space for the banquette was attained by bumping out a bay at one end of the dining room. These days, the banquette area is the couple's favorite spot for relaxing and watching TV.

"Having a big kitchen is wonderful. It makes such a difference," says Mary. "There's plenty of room now for people to gather and talk. It's probably the best design decision I've ever made."

Each year at Christmas, it's a decision that rings again of good sense. The kitchen is truly the heart of Stoney Fields—unless there are stars in the sky and snow on the ground.

Top right: *Even the red-stained barn bears its own wreath.*

Right: *An oversize antique table and raised-hearth fireplace used for cooking make the dining room a beckoning space for entertaining. A 10-foot balsam garland trimmed with dried hydrangeas decorates the table, which is flanked with new cherry Queen Anne Windsor chairs.*

Opposite: *An old post and fancy brackets define the cooktop counter, which is decorated for the holidays with hanging grapevine and bittersweet, in the remodeled kitchen. Oak flooring and "verde antique" marble counters add sophisticated country style.*

RIVER VALLEY VINTAGE

Christmas assumes a European flavor in this historic home in the Missouri River valley, where homeowners Mary and Jim Dierberg preserve the spirit of old-world Germany.

In the scenic Missouri River valley, the old German town of Hermann first beckoned to Mary and Jim Dierberg with its annual Maifest celebration of the area's historic wineries. It was a different sort of vintage, however, that drew the Dierbergs back to Hermann for keeps: a 110-year-old stone house smacking of an old-world flavor that traces to the family of German settlers who built it.

On 180 acres nestled well back from the road, the old home is at its best

Left: *An 11-foot walnut trestle table made by a St. Louis craftsman serves up savory knockwurst, bratwurst, bockwurst, and tasty cheeses for hungry holiday guests.*

Opposite: *Built in the 1880s in Hermann, Missouri, the Dierbergs' stone house with its low hip roof, symmetry, and plain facade reveals the straightforward mentality of its original German owners.*

RIVER VALLEY VINTAGE

at Christmas, when it's demurely veiled by winter's first snow. Fires blaze from its hearths, stockings await Santa, and the scent of evergreen lingers faintly in the air.

The home sparkles with good cheer reminiscent of a century ago, when the prosperous farm family that owned it would bring homemade wine up from the cellar to entertain holiday guests dancing in the ballroom. While dancers twirled and spun on the pine floors, musicians played 15 feet overhead, from a cantilevered bandstand.

The Dierbergs may not imprint the home with exactly that brand of holiday entertaining, but the overall feel—and look—they bring to the home seem plucked straight from the past.

"We are both interested in antiques," says Mary, and the couple's furnishings—especially at Christmas—are testaments to that passion. Antique toys and tree trimmings join 19th-century furniture and textiles to create a real

Above: *Beautifully trimmed with old-fashioned ornaments and encircled by antique toys, the Dierbergs' Christmas tree shares a corner of the living room with a walnut wardrobe that was locally made around 1800.*

Right: *The living room originally was two smaller rooms that Jim and Mary merged by knocking out a wall. Christmas stockings needlepointed by Mary for each of the children hang from the walnut mantel. Hand-loomed rag rugs came from a local auction.*

RIVER VALLEY VINTAGE

sense of Christmas past. Far from impairing the European character of the home, the family has underscored it with their own share of folk art.

At Christmas, this means enhancing the home's early flavor by bringing out for display charming ensembles of papier-mâché, chalkware, and cotton Santas which are enjoyed by the couple and their three children— sons, Jim and Michael, and daughter, Ellen.

Some culinary traditions of the Dierbergs also fill their house with the holiday spirit. "The whole family joins in decorating cookies in whimsical costumes and funny designs," says Mary. "It just wouldn't be Christmas without them."

After decorating gingerbread men and horse, bird, and tree cookies, the family turns to another Christmas-cookie tradition—this one, particularly appropriate for their old German

house. They bake *springerles*—small, white, square German cookies pressed with old, hand-carved molds, and *spaechtles*—large, round cookies made from a mold that has a deer carved in its center.

From its decorations to the sweet aromas of a German Christmas that waft through the air, the home remains true to old-world traditions.

Above: *Bed coverlets and many of the other antiques that fill the home's third-story attic-conversion bedroom hail from Hermann and were found by the Dierbergs at local farm sales.*

Left: *Now a bedroom for the Dierberg boys, this room originally was for entertaining guests with food and drink by the home's first owners. Whimsical antique toys and an early-1800s walnut rope bed re-create the feeling of yesteryear.*

WREATHED IN THE ROCKIES

A 200-year-old log cabin wreathed by the towering pines of the Colorado Rocky Mountains is home for the Kelly clan of Oklahoma come Christmas, when they fill it with family and fun.

When Captain John Smith built his Kentucky log cabin on land he received for serving in the American Revolution, he couldn't have known the old homestead would still be standing 200 years later—transplanted high in the Colorado Rockies.

And even had he guessed at the cabin's longevity, Smith would have been hard-pressed to imagine a more felicitous future for his humble digs than its present use as a holiday home for an expansive family from Oklahoma.

The Kelly family, headed by Vince and Ouida, is expansive in at least two senses of the word: in attitude, which is

Above: *Ouida and Vince Kelly of Tulsa moved a 200-year-old log cabin from Kentucky to Colorado's Rocky Mountains for use as their home for the holidays.*

Right: *Decorated with Christmas greens collected from nature's bounty just outside the door, the living room is comforting for the Kelly clan.*

22

WREATHED IN THE ROCKIES

convivial and open; and in number, which is steadily on the rise. Since the Kellys' seven daughters reached marrying age, the family has grown exponentially, with additions of sons-in-law and grandchildren.

Each year at Christmas the entire group gathers to share special holiday traditions in the old log structure that's chinked with a history of its own.

Furnished comfortably but informally with antiques of varying styles, the cabin exudes an unpretentious warmth that goes a long way in facilitating a quick rekindling of the ties of kinship.

"I didn't want the rooms to be too orchestrated," Ouida says. Nothing stodgy or of a single period here. Instead, the cabin is outfitted in simple finds that carry the clout of primitive power, not fine pedigree.

"I love the junk pieces, like the wooden boxes and trunks we have around here," says Ouida.

This approach to decorating means that, at the annual yuletide gathering, the family can relax and enjoy one another without constant fretting over grandchildren's whereabouts. Despite its history, the cabin is not a museum; no contents are more precious than the people.

"Spending the holidays here is more like the real Christmas—with no outside influences," says Ouida.

Vince gets even more specific: "In Colorado, our biggest decisions of the day are what color socks to put on and what's for dinner," he says.

At Christmas, though, what's for the dinner isn't a casual thought; it's an event. Ouida operates a restaurant and catering business in Tulsa; winter vacation in Colorado is an opportunity for her to cook for fun.

Christmas dinner, a collaboration between Ouida and Vince, is heavily influenced by locale; there's an unmistakable high-country taste to the meal. Colorado chukar with blue corn-bread stuffing is served with cranberry relish, fresh vegetable salad topped with Colorado goat cheese, and Red River sourdough bread—Vince's specialty.

It's a feast—and a family—that would make Captain John Smith smile at his cabin's happy fate.

Above: *The Kellys include, standing left to right: Ouida, Vince, LeAnne, Kristen, Leslie; sitting: Joe, Karen Sue, Allison, Karen Elizabeth, Carolyn.*

Opposite: *Pine and paint give the dining area informal flair.*

Below: *Vince built the bed in the master bedroom from an aspen cut on the property. Holiday decor is natural—with a distinct regional flavor.*

SOUTHERN SIDE OF THE SEASON

Atlanta's Hamilton family holds Christmas close to the heart, cocooning their home in holiday colors, cooking, and collectibles—plus the genteel Southern comforts of the season.

It's no oversight that the Atlanta home of Judy and Jack Hamilton, devoted observers of holiday tradition, dons not one Christmas light across its exterior's eaves. While other homes sparkle and shine with store-bought strings of celebratory splendor, the Hamilton home contentedly glows from within—a symbol, of sorts, of where its owners believe the real meaning of the yuletide can be found.

"We don't use any lights outside, but make it a point to keep the interior lights on during the holiday season so that the tree in the living room can be seen from outside," Jack explains. The Christmas season for the Hamiltons, then, radiates from the inside out—like all truest forms of beauty.

And just as the holiday is a time of inner meaning, it also is a time for truth. The Hamiltons symbolically express this

interpretation of the season, as well, through another decorating approach—one as natural as the manger birth itself.

Beginning with the walkway leading to the home, the family uses natural greenery as guideposts to the holiday season. Each year they festoon the porch with sweet-smelling greens tied to the posts with cheery red bows. Three dormer windows upstairs boast the same kind of organic

Above: *This Atlanta home glows from within at Christmas. Wreaths at the windows and swags along the porch set the stage for the natural holiday decorations found indoors.*

Left: *Opening onto the family room, where presents are exchanged Christmas morning, the kitchen's breakfast table is adorned with cranberries, popcorn, and dried fruit used to decorate the tree. Gingerbread men are on the tree and at the window.*

SOUTHERN SIDE OF THE SEASON

adornment—a greeting as warm as a handshake and hug to the procession of guests who visit the home during the holidays.

"I keep [the decorating] halfway simple, but still use the things that I love," says Judy.

The things Judy loves include collections of all kinds, but especially those related to Christmas. "I like decorating for every season, but I have to admit, Christmas is my favorite," she says.

Collections of antique Santas, toys, and Christmas quilts harvested throughout the years imbue the home

with a rich resonance in December—a kind of depth impossible to achieve with more casually acquired pieces.

Collecting is not solely Judy's domain, either, but a family collaboration: Jack usually adds a piece each Christmas. The couple's Christmas collectibles become especially personal, with pieces commemorating the years.

In many ways, however, each Christmas resembles the others. Continuity is assured through certain traditions that just don't change. Not one but two Christmas trees always

are decorated—one in the living room, another in the family room. Jack and Judy's sons, all three in college, try to get home in time to trim the tree or, if not, at least to join in family activities.

Christmas morning begins with the exchange of gifts, only some of which are wrapped. In Southern tradition, the remaining presents are arranged just as Santa left them—with each of the three sons' gifts lying on a chair or sofa known as their own.

A couple of dinner parties, a cookie swap with neighbors, and a

drop-in luncheon for friends busy shopping complete the holiday entertaining.

With so much enthusiasm for the

Opposite: *The living room tree is decorated with quilted ornaments, twig wreaths, red wooden hearts, and white candles. Surrounding it are Judy's collection of old toys, all encased by a green picket fence.*

Below: *The family room accommodates the tallest tree, decorated in edible treats.*

SOUTHERN SIDE
OF THE SEASON

season, the Hamiltons, not surprisingly, have decorated their home in year-round colors compatible for Christmas. The entry is painted green, and the living room is lively with red-and-white quilts and green accents.

The largest tree is decorated with dried apples, oranges, popcorn strings, and real gingerbread men—which are repeated around the kitchen windows.

Jack credits Judy for making the holidays special for the entire family. "Judy is my favorite thing about Christmas. She does it all and makes it fun."

Above: *Judy and Jack Hamilton prepare for the holidays with sons Justin and Jody (a third son, Jamie, was away on a pre-holiday ski trip).*

Right: *Decorated with bold red-and-white quilts, the living room lends itself well to a Christmas palette. Even an antique swan is given a seasonal spirit with an evergreen nest.*

Below: *Built especially for Judy, the sun-room features her favorite colors, red and white, made even more festive with feather trees.*

HALE AND HEARTY HOLIDAY

Christmas isn't just a once-a-year celebration for the Hale family of Wisconsin. Planning starts months ahead, making this home unabashedly bold for the holidays.

Above: *Homeowners Susan and Jack Hale admire reindeer cookies baked by their daughters Melissa (left) and Sarah, who sell the cookies at a local crafts fair Susan helped to organize.*

Above left: *Santa's arrival is anticipated by crazy-quilt stockings that hang above an antique cradle filled with favorite dolls from Susan's childhood.*

Opposite: *Swagged in icy signs of winter, a circa-1860s farmhouse made of fieldstone and limestone in Cedarburg, Wisconsin, is an ideal repository for a holiday wonderland indoors.*

A shaggy brow of glistening icicles fringes the eaves of the 1860s stone farmhouse in Cedarburg, Wisconsin. This, coupled with hedge-shaped mounds of snow swept off the walk to hug the home's foundation, is nature's way of setting the stage for more holiday wonderland just inside the front door.

For here, homeowner Susan Hale allows her creativity as a weaver, dollmaker, and folk-style painter to take full expression, articulating the joy of the Christmas season in tangible craft.

Susan, along with her husband, Jack, and their daughters, Melissa and Sarah, transforms the home into an old-fashioned yuletide fantasy with displays not only of her own holiday handiwork but also seasonal antiques—especially toys—and ample amounts of sweet-scented greenery.

Her Christmas dolls are scattered about the living room, sidling up to the family's collection of early Wisconsin antiques and locally made folk art. In the "blue" room, a Christmas tree sports her handmade Santas and treetop angel.

Susan's preparations aren't just for her own family's enjoyment. About 16 years ago, Susan and three fellow craftspersons got together to sell their work in a chicken coop behind Susan's home that serves as her studio. The show was a success—so much so, that it outgrew its small confines and had to move, in subsequent years, to a larger space at the Cedarburg Winery.

HALE AND HEARTY HOLIDAY

Susan is not the only member of the family to feel the flush of Christmas fever.

In past years, both daughters have shared her enthusiasm for the Christmas crafts fair. The evening before the event, Melissa and Sarah get to work themselves, heading for the kitchen where they busily bake batch after batch of giant reindeer cookies they will sell—swift as Santa's *real* reindeer—at the fair's Children's Corner.

The girls' success issues from the fact that these cookies aren't just simple cut-and-bake affairs. Each cookie is shaped with an antique cutter, then trimmed with a bell, a brightly colored ribbon, and a miniature cookie heart that is the girls' trademark.

Although Jack doesn't don an apron or wield a paintbrush or scissors in preparation for the crafts fair, he *does* head a holiday tradition of his own making—one that's a real crowd-pleaser for the entire Cedarburg community.

Jack serves as something of a choirmaster for a traveling troupe of friends and neighbors he leads on rounds of caroling.

"It started about 19 years ago as an informal get-together with friends," he says, "and it's become one of our favorite traditions."

Christmas is a time to draw close to those we love—friends, as well as family. For Jack and Susan, experiencing this closeness causes them

Above: *An old-fashioned Christmas reigns supreme in the Hales' living room, where the everyday design scheme of early Wisconsin antiques and new folk art mixes happily with Christmas dolls crafted by Susan.*

Above right: *Susan's expert eye in assembling poignant still-lifes throughout the house is responsible for the home's pervasive feeling of whimsy and warmth. In this vignette, Wisconsin antiques and locally made folk art fashion a child's fantasy.*

Right: *A menagerie of Santas and dolls made by Susan join with a car-driving Teddy and village-filled antique wagon in the family room. The Christmas tree's popcorn swags were strung by all of the members of the family; Susan made the treetop angel.*

HALE AND HEARTY HOLIDAY

to pause and reflect on their good fortune in finding true community fellowship in Cedarburg.

They came upon the community by happenstance nearly 20 years ago. "We just lucked into Cedarburg," says Susan. "We were looking for an old house, and we found one here."

More than the house became home; the Hales soon formed a deep emotional attachment to the town and its people.

"There's a real sense of caring in Cedarburg," says Susan. "Everybody's interested in historic preservation and in the arts. And Christmas here is wonderful."

The large number of old houses in Cedarburg meant that the Hales, as newcomers without much knowledge of preservation, found themselves soon swept away by a new passion.

"Living in old houses, as many of us do here, adds to our appreciation of the past," says Jack. "One of our favorite pastimes is driving around the area and discovering stone buildings."

Their own home afforded hands-on experience in preservation. At the time they bought it, the farmhouse lacked plumbing and heating—immediate priorities for the new owners.

After readying the home with structural soundness and essential modern amenities, the Hales turned to decorating. Their abiding concerns were comfort and an atmosphere compatible with the home's age.

Old-fashioned small-print wallpaper was hung over wainscoting painted a shade reminiscent of oxblood, a favorite early American color. Wood floors were spiffed up and left exposed, save for a few rag rugs strewn about for warmth. The deep window recesses—a result of the home's thick walls—were painted Williamsburg colors.

And to all of their architectural handiwork, the Hales added antiques, which they started collecting after moving in.

Surrounded by a place and people they love, no wonder the Hales' holidays are invariably hearty—and getting better all the time.

Above: *Even the kitchen is home to its share of antiques and Christmas decorations. In one corner, an antique German feather tree, dressed in a mix of old and new ornaments, stands atop an old butcher block.*

Left: *A roomy country kitchen replete with its own dining table delights the eye with a warm palette picked up from the room's original barn-red wainscoting. New cabinets were built and painted to match the wainscoting, and the entire space was brightened, giving the room a sense of spaciousness, by a red-on-cream wallpaper.*

EVERYDAY HOLIDAY

The colors of Christmas make a joyful noise in the Clifton, Virginia, home of Suzi and Travis Worsham—365 days a year. With arrival of the real holiday, the everyday atmosphere is amplified.

Above: *Built in 1907 as a summer cottage for a Washington, D.C., family, the casual feel of the Clifton, Virginia, home of Suzi and Travis Worsham proves an asset at Christmas, when holiday warmth blankets its interiors the way snow covers its grounds.*

Right: *The Worshams began updating the home by transforming an enclosed porch into a cozy yet exuberant living area. A selection of red and white tiles for the floor, a poinsettia-colored sofa, and forest green paint for the ceiling beams established a holiday palette that lasts year-round.*

Peace on earth is the intended pronouncement of red and green, the traditional colors of Christmas. But too often, December's infusion of strong holiday colors jars the home's existing palette with discordance; the balming message sounds more like a declaration of war.

Suzi Worsham, an inveterate observer and decorator of traditional Christmases, recognized the problem early on—and resolved to settle it in foolproof fashion.

If forest green and poinsettia red are the numinous colors of Christmas, she reasoned, why not design her home to employ these everyday? Why bother, in other words, with subtle pastels or other primaries that would clash with the holday hues?

Suzi put her new resolve into practice in the circa-1907 home she shares with her husband,

EVERYDAY HOLIDAY

Travis, and their three daughters, Suzanne Genevieve, Sherry Diane, and Sarah.

Originally built as a summer cottage for a Washington, D.C., family, the house was a ripe candidate for a face-lift when the Worshams purchased it in 1985. Though large enough, the home also lacked sufficient usable space to meet the needs of its new owners with their large, young family.

The first project they tackled, then, was transforming an enclosed porch into an inviting living area that, with its original, casual clapboard walls and beamed ceiling, would be ideal for the family's easygoing, informal life-style.

The jewel-toned holiday color scheme that prevails throughout the home got its start with this porch adaptation. In keeping with the space's original informality, the Worshams began furnishing it with a pair of old twig rockers, rustic but charming, that still were wearing their old green paint.

Suzi seized upon the chairs' vintage paint hue as the inspiration for a lively palette she would carry throughout the interior.

Below: *With Santas standing sentinel on the table, the Worshams enjoy a Christmas breakfast of southern specialties, including country ham with red-eye gravy and biscuits, garlic-cheese grits, homemade waffles, and fresh fruit.*

"We replaced the old tile floor with large red and white tiles and repeated the green by painting the porch ceiling," says Suzi.

Add a scarlet sofa and an antique blanket chest still donning its original green paint, and the impact is sheer drama year-round. At Christmas, the boldness is softened at the edges—tempered a bit—by a towering pine tree covered in hundreds of tiny white lights; an old stoneware pitcher of poinsettias; and liberally arranged baskets of greens gathered from the Worshams' yard.

More inviting warmth is created through the Worshams' penchant for antique furnishings. In the sunny living area, and throughout the remainder of the home, they have displayed family antiques and favorite collectibles that are an expression of both Suzi and Travis' roots. Suzi is originally from Tennessee, and Travis is a native Virginian; both have an affinity for southern furniture, as well as southern baskets and pottery, that they freely express in their home.

One of the most important rooms, especially at the holiday, is the kitchen. Suzi and Travis, by profession, are restaurateurs. At Christmas, they put their talents wholeheartedly into a succession of festive holiday meals, beginning with breakfasts, and lasting all season long.

And in surroundings that serve as a permanent palette of Christmas, everything seems to taste just a little more like the holiday in their home.

Above: *To complement the rich green and red used in other spaces, the Worshams decked their formal dining room in a jewel-toned blue, a dramatic backdrop for their collection of traditional southern antiques and family heirlooms. A late-night Christmas dessert party of southern favorites awaits their lucky guests.*

Left: *An especially loved family piece decorates one corner of the Worshams' dining room: a southern walnut corner cupboard that was given to Suzi when she was about 11 or 12 years old by her mother. Filling the cupboard is Suzi's collection of flow-blue china, Wedgwood, and early willow-pattern china.*

LIVING THE GOOD OLD DAYS

In their historic Pennsylvania farmhouse, the Ruth family re-creates the best of bygone times with a Christmas that's made special by hand and by heart.

Prudence Kinley-Ruth never really left the farm. Memories of her rural childhood lingered in the corners of her mind like the sweet fragrance of freshly mown hay on a sunny spring morning—or, every bit as pungently, like the sharp scent of sap from a snow-dappled pine just cut for Christmas.

In 1977, busy raising a family of her own with her husband, Preston, Prudence decided it was time to do more than resurrect memories: It was time to permanently install them in a home of their own.

That's exactly what the Ruths did that year when they moved into an 1881 Victorian brick house in the country, on a farm of their own. Here, they not only could keep horses (their son already was intensely interested in riding when the couple

Left: *With its blazing hearth and handcrafted Christmas decorations of dried herbs, flowers, and even garlands of squash—all made by the owner—the kitchen eating area really is the heart of the Ruths' Victorian-era home.*

Above: *An 1881 farmhouse in rural Pennsylvania recalls the bygone days of her childhood on a farm for homeowner Prudence Kinley-Ruth. When winter sweeps the tree limbs bare, the house is a stolid haven for the holidays.*

LIVING THE GOOD OLD DAYS

bought the property), but also certain other important features associated with a simpler, country life: The Ruths also could keep holidays and hopes, just the way Prudence remembered them from the past.

Christmas, especially, affords the family an opportunity to conjure up and coax into tangible place images of yesteryear. A profusion of handcrafted decorations made by Prudence and other craftspersons readies the home for the holiday, co-mingling with the warm, cinnamon scents of old-fashioned baked goods trailing from the kitchen.

Before moving to the country, Prudence had operated a small crafts shop, The Checkered Fleece, which she continued to run out of her home after the move. The array of handcrafted items made by Prudence for sale through her shop serves as a rich repository of old-style decorations for the Ruths' own home, come Christmas.

Prudence credits her rural upbringing for inspiring the assortment of crafts she creates for her cottage industry. And it is that bucolic background, too, that

Above: *The biggest and best of the Ruths' many Christmas trees fills the small parlor adjacent to the living room. Family ornaments and toys are an important part of the holiday embellishments.*

Right: *With a view of the parlor's festive Christmas tree, the living room is dedicated to comfort year-round, as well as during the holidays. An antique corner cupboard displays pewter and a favorite collection of fuzzy sheep.*

LIVING THE GOOD OLD DAYS

wields a decorative influence upon the Ruth home during the holidays.

"You don't have to be rich to have a creative, interesting home," Prudence says mildly.

One look around the old farmhouse at Christmas, and Prudence's point is well taken. If the Ruth home is anything, it is creative. And Prudence, who has raised sheep and driven a school bus "to support my country habit," declares it is not unlimited money that imbues her home with its visual interest.

Much of the creativity in the home's Christmas decor comes from Prudence's special way with dried herbs and flowers, an important part of her crafts business. Her handiwork fills virtually every room of the home as one-of-a-kind holiday wreaths and aromatic garlands.

The kitchen—the real heart of the home, according to both Preston and Prudence—is adorned with samplings of Prudence's green thumb at every turn. A handmade wreath dotted with delicate baby's breath transforms even the bland vented hood above the stove-top into a

Above: *A festive holiday "apple tree" made with apples, boxwood, and a pineapple topper symbolizing hospitality brings the season to a dining room sideboard.*

Left: *Bedecked for the season, the Ruths' dining room is the scene of many family gatherings during the holidays. A small tree in the corner of the room is laced with tiny pinecones, small wreaths covered with pickling spices, and paper angels—all handcrafted by the homeowner.*

LIVING THE GOOD OLD DAYS

bold holiday statement. Herbs strung along the fireplace, in the kitchen's intimate eating area, underscore the warmth of the crackling logs. Yet more Christmas greens, along with shiny red apples, bring yuletide color to antique pottery on the mantel.

A cupboard door shows off Prudence's talents at making barbed-wire wreaths with painted tin ornaments. Nary a single surface escapes some form of organic holiday adornment—pie safes, corner cabinets, even the tops of kitchen cabinets all are enlivened with evergreen boughs, apples, pinecones, or garlands of squash that resoundingly announce the season.

As the hub of the home, the kitchen bears a year-round palette that's ideal for Christmas costume. The original dark stain of the cabinets grew wearisome for the Ruths, so they painted all of the woodwork a subtle sage that complements the season's evergreens.

Nature's bounty is not complete without Christmas trees, and these owners have managed to squeeze an amazing number of them into their home. Decorated with handmade or keepsake ornaments and encircled by antique toys, the trees confirm what this home is about every day of the year: *living*, not longing for, the good old days.

Above: *Even a corner of the kitchen captures the essence of Christmas. With characteristic ingenuity, Prudence has tucked a tiny evergreen in a salt-glazed crock then decorated it with tin angels, patchwork hearts and cats, and woolly sheep.*

Right: *The true center of the home, the kitchen becomes far more than a work space at Christmas. Bedecked with holiday greenery that melds happily with its sage-green counters, the room is festive as well as functional.*

WISCONSIN WONDERLAND

Bejeweled in glittering snow and following the frozen bed of a meandering creek, the winding road to a century-old Wisconsin stone farmhouse is a sure path to yuletide warmth inside.

A thin curl of woodsmoke cuts the wintry air outside Cedarburg, Wisconsin, signaling a trail to the home of Jim and Sandy Pape. The chimney's offering is as functional as it is fragrant: Without this wafting warmth, the home is hard to find, tucked back from the road and concealed behind a break of pines and mulberries.

Friends visiting the Papes during the holiday season find the smoke a friendly omen, presaging what they know they will find inside: cozy contentment in front of the hearth; the kind of easy companionship and good cheer that is the real core of Christmas.

Observing tradition is a mainstay for Jim and Sandy at Christmas, and their century-old stone farmhouse with its multiple hearths and thick plastered walls provides the perfect foil.

"I really like decorating

at this time of year," says Sandy. "The house feels so old-fashioned and charming. I get out my antique ornaments—feather trees and miniature fences—and decorate each room in the house. Cedar garlands are hung over the doorways and windows, and in each window are natural wreaths which I decorate with wax ornaments, dried flowers, and rose hips."

Christmas morning begins with Jim, Sandy,

and their three children opening presents in front of the tree. The house fairly crackles with anticipation, thanks to blazing fires Jim has built, first thing, on each of the hearths.

With the last of the presents unwrapped, the family sits down to a traditional brunch that consists of Polish sausage, smoked turkey, and freshly baked bread.

As the soft sizzling and popping of the fires provide a friendly background music of

Above left: *Nearly invisible from the road thanks to a stand of pines and mulberries, the century-old stone farmhouse of Jim and Sandy Pape commands five snowy acres outside Cedarburg, Wisconsin.*

Opposite: *With its pine refectory table that seats up to 20 guests, the keeping room becomes a favorite gathering place during the holiday season.*

51

WISCONSIN WONDERLAND

sorts, another kind of warmth radiates throughout the home, too—the source being Sandy's beloved collections of antique furnishings and decorations.

Wherever possible, Sandy's tasteful eye for decorating has woven whimsical Christmas scenes amid her favorite antiques. An old Wisconsin butternut sideboard, for example, becomes a Christmas still life when adorned with a tiny antique village nestling beneath a small German feather tree. Elsewhere, small stuffed sheep from Germany— among Sandy's favorite holiday decorations— gather inside a miniature fence around another

feather tree.

And complementing the collections and furnishings is the inherent spirit of the old farmhouse itself.

"I've always loved old stone farmhouses and barns," says Sandy. "In high school I'd go to auctions with my mother and was charmed by how much character stone houses had. I suppose it's no surprise that we eventually ended up living in one."

No surprise, but a major change. Before their move to the farmhouse, Jim and Sandy had a more expected urban life-style, living and working in Milwaukee. Jim felt the tug toward independence, however, which resulted

in his buying an 1864 woolen mill in Cedarburg that he began transforming into a winery—his dream.

While Jim was getting the winery set up, his mother heard of a fieldstone farmhouse,

Above: *A Wisconsin butternut sideboard is transformed into a Christmas still life when outfitted with Sandy's antique village that nestles snugly beneath a tiny German feather tree.*

Right: *A Christmas-colored cloth from Sandy's textile collection brings seasonal festivity to a pine and butternut table lavish with holiday treats in the dining room.*

WISCONSIN WONDERLAND

complete with contents, that was going up for auction. Sandy and her mother-in-law convinced Jim to join them for the bidding on the house itself, with the provision that Sandy would not buy any of the furniture.

"We weren't really in a position to buy a home at the same time [as the business], but I felt it was worth the risk," remembers Sandy.

Jim wasn't nearly as tough an opponent as he might have been. In fact, he almost immediately shared Sandy's enthusiasm for the old home's charming stone facade, deciding, on the spot, to plunge in and take the gamble.

"I only saw the farmstead about one-half hour before the auction," says Jim. "It was in great shape and I couldn't find any cracks in the masonry. The setting was wonderful. I knew it was risky taking both places at once, but I went right ahead. It all just worked out," he recalls.

That kind of faith paid off. All that was needed to move into the home was a a good scrubbing and some fresh paint. Even shivers from winter's whistling winds weren't a problem, once Sandy's mother showed the proud owners how to "bank up" the wood-burning furnace in the cellar.

The house served the young family well, until the birth of a third child necessitated more space. The solution, a 2,000-square-foot addition designed with the help of

Jim's architect brother, Brian, more than met the growing family's needs, while preserving the original character of the historic property.

These days, the home is the restful haven that Jim and Sandy always longed for. After a snowy day of exploring the historic sites of Cedarburg, or riding a horse-drawn sleigh to the state's only remaining covered bridge just north of town, home is a great place to end the day's adventures.

"I especially enjoy a wintry evening sitting, talking, and watching the fires," says Sandy, "in the home of our dreams."

Above: *Guests are welcomed to the home in the hallway by an appliquéd St. Nicholas.*

Opposite: *Its mantel dressed for Christmas with candles, boughs, and stockings, the master bedroom's fireplace invites a long winter's nap. A personal flavor is imparted to the room by family heirlooms—the lady's rocker, needlepoint stool, and braided rug.*

Above: *Pretzels close at hand, Jim and Sandy Pape prepare for holiday guests with their children, Zack, Rachael, and Matthew.*

CHRISTMAS ALMANAC

Honoring the Christmas celebrations of the past not only keeps centuries-old traditions alive, but also adds joy and meaning to the Christmases of today.

LEGENDARY FIGURES

Traveling through many centuries and across many continents, we meet up with Santa Claus, a few of his venerable forebears, and some of his most famous chroniclers.

Christmas is a holiday of magic—and of magical characters who appear secretly in the night to grant our wishes or chasten us for our wayward ways.

The Santa Claus we cherish in this country embodies the jolliest of these characters, but in other times and in other places, his magical fellows have had much different personalities and guises, including those of a solemn old bishop and a mischievous elf.

THE GOOD SAINT NICK

Legend dates the origin of the story of Santa Claus to the fourth century, and credits the first personification of Santa to a holy man named Nicholas. Born in Asia Minor around 280 A.D., Nicholas was a devout child, entered the priesthood as a teenager, and as an adult was appointed Bishop of Myra, in what is now southwestern Turkey.

It is said that Nicholas was a benevolent and charitable man, and after his death, he was made a saint for the many miracles he performed. He died on December 6 in the first half of the fourth century; the anniversary of his death became a feast day on the church calendar.

The stories of Nicholas' kindliness earned him the adoration of medieval Christians throughout the world. His devotees extended from his homeland through Russia and into western Europe. Eventually, Nicholas became patron saint of many people, among them seafarers, children, tailors, merchants, travelers, and maidens of marrying age.

St. Nicholas was so revered that even the Protestant Reformation of the 16th century could not fully diminish his status. But because the Reformation abolished the

worship of saints, Nicholas' followers began calling him a secular saint instead of a religious one. They honored Nicholas' generosity by giving gifts, particularly to children. Many claimed that St. Nicholas roamed the earth on his feast day every year, leaving sweets and trinkets in children's shoes.

A FOLK HERO IN MANY LANDS

The tale of the wandering gift-giver begun with St. Nicholas proved to have universal appeal. Gradually, similar tales were adopted by many countries, where they were revised to fit national customs and are still told and retold today.

In Holland, for example, it is said that on December 6, St. Nick arrives aboard a ship— appropriate for a nation that lives intimately with the sea. Once ashore, he mounts a white horse to deliver his gifts to the children.

In England, the story of St. Nicholas was woven with pagan tales from the country's Celtic heritage. There, it is Father Christmas, who, with fur cloaks draped across thin shoulders and a holly crown atop his long hair, appears on December 24, cradling a bowl of wassail in his arms.

In Germany, some children wait for St. Nick to arrive on his white steed, while others look for an aged, white-bearded *Weihnachtsmann* (Christmas Man) riding through the heavens in a chariot drawn by two white goats. Still others anticipate the coming of the *Christkindl* (Little Christ Child), an angelic servant sent by the Holy Infant. (When German immigrants settled in Pennsylvania, they gave *Christkindl* an American name, Kris Kringle. Kris

traveled astride a mule and left gifts in baskets.)

The Scandinavian gift bearer is a little elf— reflective of the many folk tales of trolls and gnomes held dear in the Norse lands. The Christmas elf has various names: Norwegians receive presents from *Julesvenn,* the Danes have their *Julenisse,* and the Swedes welcome *Jultomten.* By whatever name they give him, Scandinavian children know this elf to be an impish character who needs cajoling. To that end, they set out bowls of hot porridge to entice him into their homes, hoping that he'll leave them gifts in return.

ST. NICK'S UNFRIENDLY COMPANION

Many of the early folk tales about St. Nicholas included an evil character, as well, whose presence represented the threat of punishment, considered a great deterrent to bad behavior.

This malevolent counterpart to the good St. Nick neither brought gifts nor spread good cheer. His name and mode of dress changed from one country to the next, but his role always was the same: to terrorize children whose conduct was found wanting by flicking a switch or threatening to carry them away in a sack.

In Holland, this fearsome creature was known as *Swarte Piet,* or Black Pete. Black Pete was a Moorish figure who reflected the Dutch's unhappy history under Spanish rule.

In Germanic countries, children knew this anti-hero as *Krampas, Hans Trapp,* or *Schmutzli,* a creature with devil-like

LEGENDARY FIGURES

horns and a masked face—a reincarnation of pagan demons of ancient tales.

One malevolent figure in these stories is seen as St. Nicholas' alter ego. It is believed that those who opposed the celebration of Saint Nicholas conjured this scary character to lessen his appeal. *Pelz-Nikolaus,* or Nicholas-in-Fur, seemed angry with his evil, fiery eyes and long red tongue. He dressed in dirty furs and rags—and no doubt terrorized children wherever he roamed.

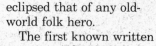

ST. NICK IN THE NEW WORLD

Immigrants to the new world brought with them the tales of St. Nick from their various homelands. Each ethnic group clung to its own traditional story for many years. The Dutch, who began settling New York in the 1620s, honored their *Sinterklaas;* German immigrants of the 18th century brought to the Mid-Atlantic region their *Pelz-Nikolaus* and the *Christkindl.* Meanwhile, the Puritan settlers of New England eschewed any Christmas figure—indeed, any celebration of the holiday—as blasphemous.

But by the early 1800s, holiday customs were beginning to merge across ethnic boundaries, and eventually, the stories were combined to create one new one. This story would become the tale of Santa Claus, a national Christmas figure whose importance in the minds of American children

eclipsed that of any old-world folk hero.

The first known written mention of St. Nicholas' American cousin appeared in 1809, when Washington Irving, one of America's foremost authors, wrote a satire of New York and its residents under the pseudonym Diedrich Knickerbocker.

In *A History of New York from the Beginning of the World to the End of the Dutch Dynasty,* Irving mentions St. Nicholas

some 20 times. Unlike his old-world forebears, Irving's St. Nick was not a churchly personage in bishop's robes, but rather a jovial Dutch burgher wearing breeches and a broad-brimmed hat and smoking a long clay pipe. He rode over rooftops in a wagon, pulling presents from his pockets and dropping them down the chimneys of houses where good girls and boys lived.

The following year, another image of St. Nick was created when the

New York Historical Society paid homage to the ethnic heritage of New York with a dinner honoring St. Nicholas. To mark the event, an artist designed a woodcut depicting a dour St. Nick with a smiling little girl whose apron bulged with toys and a weeping little boy with a switch stuck in his buttonhole. The illustration, the earliest American rendering of St. Nick, was paired with a poem about "Sancte Claus."

A JOLLY OLD ELF

Several years after Irving's *A History of New York* was published, Clement C. Moore, a New York linguist, clergyman, and father of nine, offered his embellishments to the American tale. In December of 1822, after spending the day shopping with a neighborhood handyman—a chubby, white-bearded Dutchman—Moore penned a special holiday gift for his 6-year-old daughter.

In only a few hours, he wrote "A Visit from Saint Nicholas," a 56-line poem into which he wove bits of folklore, contemporary literature (including allusions to Irving's *History*), and the image of his friend the handyman. The verses, rich in visual imagery, paint a portrait of a dimple-cheeked, twinkle-eyed elf with a miniature sleigh pulled by eight tiny reindeer.

Moore intended this work, which he called "Twas the night before Christmas," only as entertainment for his daughter. However, the child was so delighted with it that she shared the poem with a family friend. The next year, the poem was printed anonymously in a Troy, New York, newspaper. For years afterward, the poem appeared in an ever-growing number of periodicals. Moore finally admitted authorship in 1837, when the work was included in a volume of poetry.

The poem was reprinted in numerous books and magazines, and provided inspiration to many an artist, who illustrated the vivid scenes the poem suggested. Here was St. Nick descending a chimney, flying over rooftops in his sleigh, and happily filling stockings hung by the fireplace.

Some artists drew St. Nick in the image of the Nordic god Thor, thundering through the

heavens; others illustrated the character as a little Irish leprechaun.

The most memorable and enduring images, however, were those conceived by Thomas Nast, a Bavarian-born artist whose first Santa was published in the early 1860s, in a Christmas anthology containing Moore's poem.

Nast drew Santa Claus and other Christmas subjects for 23 years while employed by *Harper's Weekly*, where he'd made his name as a political cartoonist and Civil War illustrator.

His first holiday pictures for the magazine appeared in 1863. They included Santa in tableaus of Union soldiers at camp and at home on furlough. Nast later depicted Santa making

toys at his workshop and relaxing with his pipe before a fireplace.

Like Moore, Nast created a plump, lovable gnome with a cheerful expression and a downy beard. Nast added a bushy handlebar moustache, dressed Santa in a wooly, fur-trimmed suit and cap, and gave him a bundle bursting with toys. This Santa good-naturedly accepted hugs and kisses from adoring children.

By the turn of the century, it was Nast's friendly figure who traveled the earth on Christmas Eve to reward good little girls and boys. And it is Nast's Santa who lives today, firmly fixed in the Christmas fantasies of most of America.

CUSTOMS AND TRADITIONS

The holiday traditions we hold most dear—though born of age-old legends and beliefs whose origins have faded—provide a festive, colorful, noisy link to the past.

Our celebration of Christmas is a joyful jumble of customs that developed in many different lands, over many thousands of years. Woven into our celebrations are vestiges of ancient Roman festivals and early Christian practices, of medieval pagan rituals, and of Victorian nostalgia.

MAKE A JOYFUL NOISE

One of the earliest and most pervasive customs at Christmastime is noise-making. The custom's origins are pagan: It was once believed that creating a dreadful din would frighten away evil spirits lurking in the dark and cold of winter. But cacophonous noisemaking—both innocent and fun as it was—also was held dear by Christian celebrants.

In colonial times, Christmas Eve revelers marched through the streets blowing horns and tin whistles, shouting, jingling bells, and beating drums. Householders often threw out coins in response—either to acknowledge the noisemakers for their service or simply to make them leave and take their noise elsewhere.

This boisterous tradition had its detractors, those who found little more in the practice than a noisy nuisance. By the late 1800s, laws were created to keep the noisemaking out of the streets.

The Boar's Head   The Wassail Bowl

Throughout the country, and particularly in the South, firearms and fireworks were a favorite and legal means for raising a racket. Neighbors separated by vast plantation acreages saluted one another on Christmas Day with a resonant report of rifles. Other amateur artillerists took great delight in the sputters and sparks of rockets, Roman candles, and other mini-explosives, as well as in their effect on young ladies, who could be made to shriek when firecrackers landed at their feet.

Those who couldn't afford to purchase such fireworks made their own, inflating hog bladders to toss into a fire for an impressive blast, or drilling blacksmiths' anvils and loading them

with gunpowder to create a boom as powerful and fearsome as a cannon's.

A slightly more refined form of noisemaking was the annual Christmas shoot, which brought marksmen together of an afternoon to test their skills for monetary stakes. Many competitors were members of target-shooting clubs, and added to the spirit of ceremony by dressing in old military uniforms, marching through the streets with a brass band, and concluding their shooting matches with feasting and dancing.

While adults and older children made this clamor out of doors, youngsters made their own share of celebratory noise inside the house. A favorite turn-of-the-century noisemaker for children

was called a cricket, a little tin saucer-shaped device with a springy steel tongue that chirped when squeezed—driving adults to distraction.

Slightly less noisy and less annoying, perhaps, was the cracker, a tube of colorful tissue filled with a treat or trinket: a false moustache or a toy pipe, for example. When the ends of the tube were tugged apart, the cracker burst with a bang. (Crackers were invented by an English confectioner in the mid-1800s. The first crackers made no noise, but neither did they inspire many sales. So the same confectioner packed each tube with a chemically treated paper strip that popped under friction. A new and noisy tradition was born.)

SWEETER SOUNDS OF THE SEASON

More pleasing and harmonic noises come at year's end in the form of carols. From medieval times, carols have carried on the glad tidings of Christmas. The word originally meant a circle dance accompanied by song. Unlike the solemn Latin hymns and chants written for the church, carols were secular, joyful tunes sung in native languages so they could be enjoyed by common folk.

Eventually, the simple melodies of carols and the solemn words of liturgical music were woven together into songs that celebrated the Christ child's birth. The earliest Christmas carols may

CUSTOMS AND TRADITIONS

have been sung around 1223, when St. Francis of Assisi arranged the first manger scene in Italy. Those who visited the crèche are said to have sung carols that told the story of the Nativity.

Since the 13th century, hundreds of carols in various forms, including lullabies, marches, and ballads, have been sung and passed along from one generation to the next. Some were composed by poets, minstrels, and clerics; others evolved as singers put words to ancient instrumental music, or composed new lyrics for existing folk tunes and hymns.

The specific origins of many of the Christmas carols sung today—including the 16th-century "God Rest Ye Merry, Gentlemen," and the 17th-century "The First Noel"—are unknown. Others have traceable lineage. The melody for "Joy to the World," for example, was derived from Handel's *Messiah,* and "What Child Is This?" was first popularly known in England as "Greensleeves."

Some of today's most popular songs are not religious at all, but rather celebrate the secular aspects of the season. "O Tanenbaum," for example, is Germany's homage to the Christmas tree. "Deck the Halls" is an old Welsh song that revels in the hanging of the greens.

HERE WE COME A-CAROLING
The tradition of caroling is that of the wandering minstrels. As early as the 1400s, for example, many carols were sung by English men and women who performed in exchange for coins for the needy.

Later, the custom of caroling was adapted by English night watchmen, or waits, who sang while making their rounds at holiday time. When night watches were eliminated, carolers continued to walk the streets simply for their own enjoyment and for the entertainment of their listeners.

In this country, the singing of carols was limited to church services until about 100 years ago. It was then that the American practice of singing door to door was begun—adapted, perhaps, from the English watchmen's traditional singing.

KEEPING THE CAROLS ALIVE
Like other early folk songs, carols were preserved orally, passed along for centuries before they were ever written down.

But when the celebration of Christmas

was banned in England under the 17th-century rule of Puritan Oliver Cromwell, carols and caroling were in danger of disappearing in that country, and on the Continent as well. Carols might have been lost forever, were it not for a secular interest in antiquity that kept them alive for nearly 200 years, if only for singing in private.

When inexpensive printing processes were developed in the 1800s, historians began publishing their private collections of traditional carols in books, reawakening enthusiasm for this music.

Publishing inspired a renewed interest in old carols, and the composition of a choir of new songs, as well. Some of these more recent compositions carry with them the tales of their origins. In 1818, for example, "Silent Night" was written in Austria by parish priest Josef Mohr and church organist Franz Gruber when the church organ malfunctioned on Christmas

Eve. Mohr hastily wrote a song to replace the customary Christmas organ music and asked Gruber to pick out a guitar accompaniment. (An organ repairman is credited with helping to spread the carol to other congregations.)

And in 1863, poet Henry Wadsworth Longfellow expressed his anguish over the Civil War and his hope for peace on earth with the words to "I Heard the Bells on Christmas Day." It is said Longfellow was inspired by the wounding of his son in the Battle of Gettysburg.

Episcopal minister Phillip Brooks composed the words to "O Little Town of Bethlehem" in 1868 to commemorate his trip to that holy site three years earlier.

QUIETER CUSTOMS

The Christmas season has inspired many noiseless traditions, as well, of course. Many were adapted from pagan or secular customs. Here are but a few of them. Many are still honored in various regions of the country; a few live only in stories of early celebrations.

SILENT NIGHT, BURNING BRIGHT

Burning a yule log is reminiscent of the Nordic mid-winter festival *Juul,* when bonfires were lit in

prayer for the sun's return. As a Christmas symbol, the bonfire was reduced to a single log, lit on Christmas Eve with a branch from the previous year's log.

For luck, the blaze was kept alive at least through Christmas Day and, in many homes, until Epiphany on January 6. This practice was honored in the 19th-century

American South, where work on the plantations halted while the yule log burned.

Wassailing is an old English tradition. The word wassail is derived from an Anglo-Saxon toast, *waes hael,* meaning "be whole." It's also the name for a drink made of hot spiced ale or wine and baked apples.

At early English Christmas celebrations, a bowl of wassail was passed for everyone to sip from. An empty wassail bowl was carried around the village by those begging for charity and by carolers, as well, so that listeners could express their appreciation by replenishing it. (Hence one carol with two titles, "Here We Come A-Wassailing" or "Here We Come A-Caroling").

On Epiphany, the wassail bowl might be taken to an apple orchard, where its contents were sprinkled on tree roots to ensure a bountiful crop in the coming year.

MAKING MERRY WITH MUMMERY AND BELSNICKLING

Also from England comes the custom of mummery, a popular entertainment that seems to have begun sometime during the 14th century. On Christmas Eve, groups of villagers would blacken or mask their faces and roam the

CUSTOMS AND TRADITIONS

streets, dancing and carousing in return for coins from delighted onlookers.

Mummery also took the form of short skits that portrayed either the victory of good over evil or the resurrection of life. One well-known play called for the hero, St. George, to battle a villain to the death; the slain victim then was revived, miraculously, by a doctor.

English immigrants brought mummery to America; it remained popular here until the mid-1800s. American mummery more often was musical than theatrical: Masked mummers paraded through communities, singing songs or reciting verses. Sometimes they performed the play with George Washington rather than the English St. George as the hero.

Similar to mummery was belsnickling, a custom popular into the first part of this century among the German immigrants of Pennsylvania. "Belsnickle" is a corruption of *Pelz-Nikolaus,* the name given to one of St. Nick's fearsome companions. Belsnicklers were dressed in dirty furs and rags and gruesomely made up. Carrying treats and a whip, a Belsnickle visited country homes, rewarding good children with candies and frightening naughty children with sharp snaps of the switch.

'TIS BETTER TO GIVE...

The tradition of exchanging gifts at Christmas began with the story of the Three Magi,

who offered the Christ child gold, frankincense, and myrrh.

Giving has since worked its way into many seasonal stories. St. Nicholas and most of his counterparts were known for their charity. Giving gifts in their honor originated around the 1200s, when provincial French nuns brought presents to poor children's homes on the eve of December 6, St. Nicholas' feast day.

In some European countries, presents are still given in his name on December 5 or 6; most gifts, however, are exchanged under the guise of St. Nick's current incarnation, Santa Claus, on December 24 or 25.

When the gift-giving custom caught on across the Atlantic, Americans exchanged such

traditional presents as money and foodstuffs—particularly fruits, nuts, and sweets. In the 1700s, at the Moravian settlement in Bethlehem, Pennsylvania, for example, everyone in the community received apples for Christmas.

Nonfood gifts tended toward the utilitarian: a handkerchief or a hand-knitted scarf. Even a length of rope was a suitable present gratefully received. A Lutheran minister noted in his journal in 1799 that he had received just such a gift.

For children, there was a modest assortment of toys. Before the Industrial Revolution, most playthings were homemade. A rag doll or a hand-carved animal was considered a great treasure. Well-to-do

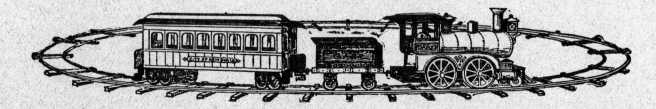

families could order manufactured toys from Europe, as George Washington did for his stepchildren in 1759. The mails were not reliable, however, and the wax doll, tea set, and toy soldier Washington requested for his children in September failed to arrive until March of the following year.

... AND THE GIFTING GROWS

By the mid-1800s, factory-made products were becoming more available to the public. From mechanical trains to pocket watches to silk robes, Americans had more choices for gift giving than ever before, and the goods filled new department stores such as R.H. Macy's.

Shopping for Christmas gifts became a custom in its own right, one that has grown through the decades. Early shoppers suffered many of the same plights as today's shoppers: lining up at crowded cashiers, jostling fellow package-laden shoppers, and getting stuck in holiday traffic jams of horse-drawn carriages.

Why do we leave carrots and apples for Santa's reindeer? Offering goodies to Dasher and Dancer and the rest of the team provides a symbolic means to carry on an old custom of kindness.

Treating animals at Christmas was a tradition of long standing in Europe, where farm families often would give extra rations to their livestock and toss out scraps for wild animals.

Scandinavian immigrants in America carried on their native custom of providing oat or wheat sheaves for the birds. German settlers often decked a tree in the yard with vegetables, fruits, nuts, and bread.

TREES AND TRIMMINGS

*For turn-of-the-century Americans, holiday greens—the balsam and
the spruce, the holly and the ivy, and the mistletoe—held the promise
of a joyful and festive season.*

ecking the
halls is a
venerable
custom of
ancient origins. Today the
presence of evergreens
evokes the very spirit of
the holiday season.

For centuries,
evergreens were believed
to have mysterious
powers. That they
remained verdant
throughout the winter,
when all plants around
them died, seemed
somehow supernatural to
ancient peoples. The
green leaves and needles,
the berries, and the cones
not only held the promise
that spring would return,
but symbolized the
continuance of life, even
in the midst of death.

THE HANGING
OF THE GREENS

The seasonal celebration
of greens can be traced to
centuries-old pagan
rituals, from which many
of our Christmas
traditions evolved. In

Roman times, celebrants
brought greenery indoors
to bring vitality—and
welcome fragrances—into
their homes during the
dead of winter.

As Christianity and the
celebration of Christmas
grew, so did the use of
greens to decorate both
church and home.
Eventually, any part of a
home might be adorned
with laurel, yew, ivy,
hemlock, and bay.

In America's younger
days, many early settlers,
influenced by Puritan
beliefs that celebration
was inappropriate for
religious events, chose to
avoid greens as decor.
However, a melding of
European traditions and,
eventually, a Victorian
love for ornamentation
brought greens into most
American homes.

In the 19th century,
evergreens were used to
honor the deceased at
Christmastime. The
bereaved wove wreaths,
crowns, stars, and crosses
to lay in cemeteries.
Later, they brought the
greens indoors. They

found that the greens
filled their homes
with a festive spirit;
they also were grateful
for the powerful
potpourris the decor
brought to rooms made
stale from lack of
fresh air.

Greens sculptures were
combined with variegated
ropes twisted from laurel
and pine. The garlands
were draped wherever
possible: over doors, along
stair rails, under and over
windows, and around
picture frames.

A Brief History Of the Tree

Though trees are significant in our celebrations of Christmas today, they are more recent additions to the holiday than wreaths and garlands. In Roman times, trees were brought inside and simply adorned to create shelters for kindly deities.

It was much later that the evergreen tree was adopted as a symbol of Christianity. Legend has it that, in the eighth century, an English monk traveled to Germany to spread the word of God. When he happened upon an oak tree where a human sacrifice was to take place, he stopped the sacrifice, chopped down the oak, and found a young fir growing between its roots. The missionary took this as a sign that Christianity would replace paganism in the world, and dedicated the fir tree to the Holy Infant.

The first decorated trees associated with Christmas appeared in the Middle Ages as part of miracle plays, public dramas that were performed to help instruct a largely illiterate populace in the tenets of their faith.

One of the plays staged in late December reenacted Adam and Eve's expulsion from the Garden. A tree, hung either with real or paper apples to represent the Tree of Knowledge, often served as the play's only prop.

Miracle plays eventually fell out of favor. Though the practice of decorating a tree to symbolize Christianity did not, Christmas trees still were not widely used in Europe until the 16th or 17th century. The earliest known record of a decorated tree comes from Alsace. There, in 1605, a writer noted how local residents trimmed fir trees with apples, paper roses, sweets, gold foil, and wafers that represented the Eucharist.

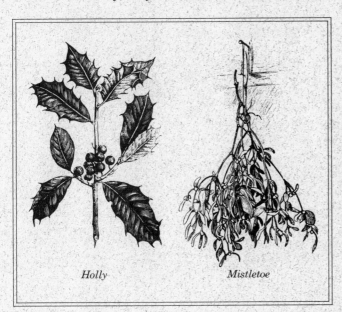

Holly   *Mistletoe*

TREES AND TRIMMINGS

LIGHTING THE TREE

Among the earliest ornamentation for the Christmas tree was candlelight. Martin Luther may have been one of the first to have adorned a Christmas tree with candles. Luther, it is said, went wandering in the forest one clear 16th-century Christmas Eve night. He was so touched by the sight of the stars sparkling through the trees that he wanted to somehow share it with his children. He chopped down a fir, brought it home, and decorated it with candles to represent that starlight.

Many years would pass before the first written reference to candlelit trees appeared. It was in 1708, when a German-born member of Louis XIV's court wrote a letter reminiscing about her childhood Christmases, and mentioned the box-wood trees with candles fastened to each branch.

Sometimes candles were not put on the tree at all, but rather alongside it—arranged on a *lichtstock*, or light deck. This German creation was a simple wooden pyramid structure, decorated with evergreens, Nativity figurines, fruits, and flowers, and adorned with dozens of candles.

THE ROYAL TREE

Throughout the 18th century, the Christmas tree—already much-used in Germany—gained acceptance across Europe.

Decorating a tree was considered a charming custom in England. Two German-born members of the English royal family, Queen Charlotte and Queen Adelaide, enjoyed trees in the late 18th and early 19th centuries. Queen Victoria's consort, Albert, also of German heritage, brought a Christmas tree to Windsor Castle in 1841. Recorded by an engraving in the *Illustrated London News* several years later, their handsome tabletop tree was decked with tapers, baskets of sweets, and gingerbread. Victoria's subjects wasted little time in emulating their beloved monarch by decorating their own trees.

THE TREE IN AMERICA

It was German settlers who brought the tradition of Christmas trees to this country. The enthusiasm for the tree grew in part thanks to admiration for Queen Victoria, which inspired Americans to follow English fashion. When an engraving of the queen's Christmas tree appeared in 1850 in *Godey's Lady's Book*, a widely read monthly magazine, the tree as part of American Christmases seemed destined for posterity.

However, until the last half of the 19th century, putting up a tree was still an unusual custom. There are some published reports of trees from various Pennsylvania communities—where there was a large Germanic population—beginning in the 1820s.

In 1823, the York *Gazette* noted that a society of bachelors gave to a group of old maids a little Christmas tree in exchange for "one Cart load of Gingercakes." *The*

Saturday Evening Post, a venerable Philadelphia periodical, spoke glowingly in 1825 of trees decorated with fruits "richer than the golden apples of Hesperides, or the sparkling diamonds . . . in the wonderful cave of Aladdin."

Most Christmas trees in 19th-century America were small enough to fit on a table—important because, until manufactured metal stands became available in the 1870s, trees were supported in tubs filled with sand, coal, or rocks, or were nailed to boards. Only short, light specimens could be held safely with such bases.

THE TREE ADORNED

German settlers carried their tradition of trees with them wherever they went in the new land, and by the turn of this century, most Americans had adopted the custom. By that time, if they didn't have a tree for their own home, most families had one nearby, in a church or school, that they could enjoy.

In the early 1900s, trees were meant mostly for children, some of whom believed that Santa brought trees and trimmings in his sleigh. Parents decorated the tree and kept it hidden from the children until late Christmas Eve or early Christmas morning. It was with great ceremony that the tree was finally revealed in all its glory.

Surely the tree must have been a magical sight to childish eyes. The boughs were heavy with precious things: Amid tapered candles were hung intricate paper cutouts, cookies, pieces of taffy, tiny toys, gilded

ornaments, strings of popcorn and cranberries, ribbon bows, and dried flowers. At the peak a delicate angel floated or a gilded star sparkled. (Manufactured decorations, though somewhat available in the late 1800s, didn't affect American tree decorating until later in this century.)

Gifts also were part of the decorations. Small wrapped packaged were fastened to the branches with colorful strings or ribbons, then removed and opened on Christmas Day.

Once decorated, the tree was left standing for the full 12 days of Christmas, then taken down on January 6, the Epiphany. Edible ornaments were left hanging until then, when they offered sweet consolation for the removal of the beautiful tree.

TREES AND TRIMMINGS

A New American Business

As decorating for Christmas grew, endorsed and popularized by contemporary periodicals, the demand for suitable evergreens also grew.

There was no shortage of greens in the countryside, where any family could cut down their own tree. In the burgeoning cities, however, trees and greens were difficult to come by. The shortage seemed only to create another avenue for American ingenuity to show itself.

In 1851, an enterprising woodsman named Mark Carr, who lived in the Catskill Mountains, recognized the market for trees in New York City. So he filled two ox-sleds with fresh-cut spruces and firs from the forests around his home and shipped them by steamer to the city, thus establishing the first Christmas tree lot in America.

At the bustling Washington Market in lower Manhattan, Carr sold out his entire stock in short order. He returned the following year with even more trees.

Thirty years later, more than 600 other dealers had followed Carr's lead, selling hundreds of thousands of specimens imported by wagons, ships, and trains from across the Northeast.

Other cities in the late 19th century benefited from the initiative of entrepreneurs like Carr.

In Washington, D.C., holly and evergreen trees from Maryland and Virginia were sold at the large Centre Market. In Chicago, trees were ferried from Wisconsin and Michigan to be sold along the urban lakefront.

At the turn of the century, a New Jersey farmer gambled that Christmas tree lovers might also flock to a "living" market. He planted the first tree farm, with about 25,000 Norway spruce. Customers, most of them from nearby Trenton, selected trees in the field. They could carry the trees away with them or have them delivered by horse-drawn wagon—for the price of $1.

Breaking with Tradition

Rather than buying or cutting a new tree, some thrifty families recycled their trees from one year to the next. Many a housewife stripped the dried evergreen needles

off the tree when the holidays were over and wrapped the bare limbs with white cotton batting. The tree, carefully covered with newspaper, was then stored until the next Christmas, when the bare branches were set up again and redecorated.

When there were no evergreens—last year's or fresh—available, revelers made do with whatever they could find. West-roving pioneers, for example, put up cottonwood or sassafras trees, and adorned their homes with sagebrush and sunflowers.

MERRY MISTLETOE AND THE HOLLY AND THE IVY

Though every child waited eagerly to see what the Christmas tree would hold, it was mistletoe that caught the interest of older revelers.

In ancient days, mistletoe was sacred to the Druids, holy men in the early Celtic culture. They believed it offered protection from evil and ensured fertility. In mid-winter ceremonies, they cut mistletoe and offered it to their gods; they also distributed sprigs of mistletoe among the people to hang over the entrances to their home.

Centuries later, mistletoe still was credited with mysterious powers, and was hung to inspire significant Christmas kisses. Though many in 19th-century America thought the practice uncivilized, it was an essential convention in the festivities of English immigrants. And, in fact, according to British superstition, a young woman not kissed under the mistletoe would not be married the following year. The best mistletoe was believed to be that grown in England—at twice the cost of its American cousin. But fathers with daughters of a marrying age were willing to pay the price.

The mistletoe was wound around wooden hoops to make "kissing boughs," adorned with figurines, fruits, and ribbons. The boughs were hung in a well-trafficked location in the house to ensure their greatest use.

Also imported from England was much of the holly used in wreaths, in garlands, and tied into swags. Like mistletoe, holly was once believed to contain protective powers. Later, in the Anglican Church, holly became associated with the Crucifixion, its red berries symbolic of the suffering of Christ.

Whatever their significance, the bright berries were treasured by early holiday decorators. Each year the sprig of holly with the reddest berries was reserved for the top of the Christmas pudding. Other branches were arranged in vases like flowers, surrounded by the delicate vines of ivy. Ivy is an ancient symbol of love, and since the Middle Ages it's been included in traditional European—and now American—decor.

COLLECTOR'S CHRISTMAS

Christmas collectibles from the past—games, puzzles, books, toys, ornaments, candle holders, and tree lights—bring a heady nostalgia to the holiday, at heart and in the home.

GIFT BEARERS

The most popular secular symbol of Christmas, Santa has been cherished for nearly 200 years. The materials from which he has been crafted have changed over time, but his role as gift bearer has not.

Whether driving a fashionable car or steering a traditional sleigh, Santa always arrived at his destination laden with toys and a decorated Christmas tree. One of the most beloved symbols of the holiday, this gift bearer appeared as a candy container, a table decoration, and even a treetop ornament.

Most of the early Santa figures were constructed of papier-mâché, made in Germany, and usually known as Belsnickles, which means St. Nicholas dressed in fur (see page 138). Germans in the Thuringen region had learned the secret of papier-mâché from a French soldier following the Thirty Years War.

Above: *Dressed in flannel suits and trimmed in rabbit fur, these toy-laden early 1920s Santas speed to their destinations.*

Right: Weihnachtsmann *carrying feather trees, baskets, and sacks of toys vary in date from 1880 to just before World War I. Santa's sleigh is being pulled by a cloth-covered composition reindeer.*

GIFT BEARERS

For the earliest Belsnickles, artisans created clay models from which negative molds were made. The figures were varnished and painted. "Dot" pupil painted eyes, black lid lining, and one-stroke brows in reddish brown are characteristic of these early figures.

Switches or feather branches were put into the arms of many Santas. Rabbit-fur beards, chenille trim, and mica chips often further embellished the more lavish figures. Red and white were the most common clothing colors. Green, lavender, pale pink, and blue clothing was uncommon; black and somber-colored clothing was rare.

Old Belsnickles tend to be expensive today. Increasing their value is a flat or turban-style hat, a multicolored robe, unusual fur trim, or a child or animal held in

the gift bearer's arms. Size also increases a Belsnickle's worth: figures more than 13 inches tall are rare.

Early Belsnickles— those made prior to World War I—were heavier in composition and had more facial detail than later figures. After the 1920s, Belsnickles were lighter weight and had thinner construction.

Right: *Carrying his lantern to light the way, this early wood-jointed Weihnachtsmann was molded entirely from papier-mâché.*

Below: *Unusual examples of Father Christmas include Santa on a donkey and a lavish red-and-white-striped, fur-dressed Santa.*

Opposite: *Stern-faced Belsnickles from 1870 to 1900 carry switches or feather branches.*

In Germany around 1835, the Weihnachtsmann first appeared. As a result of the Reformation and Martin Luther, St. Nicholas soon became "the nice old man" in the village who delivered presents to good little boys and girls. Belsnickles made the transition to the personage of a kind, elderly figure. Rather than switches or a miniature feather tree, these papier-mâché figures often carried bags and baskets of toys and gifts. Even though Belsnickles were still in existence, Protestants preferred Weihnachtsmann as their symbol of the gift bearer.

Weihnachtsmann originally were made from papier-mâché and wax, later from composition, which is similar to papier mâché. Composition-based Santas have their roots in the 1880s, when Germans manufactured papier-mâché dolls heads dipped into liquid plaster. Composition ingredients included dissolved paper, a glue solution, chalk, heavy spar, and plaster or clay. Pressed into a two-part mold, the resulting figure was dried, then dipped in wax or plaster, and ultimately painted.

Finely detailed, these plastered figures had ruddy complexions and stooped postures, and they often carried miniature feather trees and toys.

Few Santas were waxed, and few were full figures. Most were only molded heads, arms, and boots. The parts, which often could be bent, were attached to a core, frequently a hollow cardboard candy container.

The rarest composition figures wore blue, black, or brown; the more common dressed in red. At the turn of the century, felt replaced flannel as the material for clothing.

Later, after World War I, leather belts were used in lieu of threaded cords. Rabbit fur and lamb's wool were used as trim for clothes, and rabbit fur was used for beards. Early Santas had the fur attached directly to their faces. In later years, however, the fur was attached to a piece of adhesive tape and then glued onto the plaster-coated face.

Another type of Santa—one that's extremely rare today—is the chalkware Santa made by the Pennsylvania Dutch. Formed in molds filled with a thin mixture of plaster of paris, these Santas had a somber appearance, with stern faces and snow-trimmed coats of blue and brown.

Whether a pull toy, a candy container, or a tree or table decoration, Santa is assured a warm place in the hearts of young and old who need to believe in the one bearing gifts of peace and love.

GLASS ORNAMENTS

Hand-blown glass baubles from Germany—created throughout the 19th century—have survived to become a charming, highly collectible addition to the Christmas tree in many American homes.

With brilliant splendor, antique glass baubles continue to serve as reflective reminders of old-world charm and craftsmanship on scores of Christmas trees in America.

The best of these hand-blown ornaments hail from Lauscha, Germany, where Europe's leading glassblowers fled from their homeland of Swabia to escape religious persecution for their Lutheran beliefs.

Lauscha's success as a glassblowing center resulted primarily from two large families who settled there: the Greniers and the Mullers. The development of the art of glassblowing, in fact, traces to two members of these original families: George Greiner, who invented a forge in 1820, and Ludwig Muller, who improved it.

Among the earliest blown baubles were *kugels,* distinguished by their heavy weight and ornate brass hanger. A kugel, German for "a round or ball shape," ranges in size from under 1 inch to up to 14 inches in diameter. Silver spheres as well as grape clusters, teardrops, and pear-shaped ornaments were blown in hues of red, silver, blue, green, and amethyst.

During the second half of the 1800s, however, innovations made the kugel obsolete. In 1867, the Lauscha glassblowers built a gas depot to provide a constant gas flame that was adjustable and extremely hot, enabling the production of thin-walled bubbles of glass. In 1870, Louis

Opposite: A tree is resplendent with ornaments made from 1870 to 1939. Those fashioned from glass sparkle brighter, thus their popularity over ornaments of other types.

Above: *Crowned with a brass Victorian top, kugels blown from 1860 to 1890 in hues of bright, vibrant colors graced American Christmas trees.*

Right: *Pre-World War I extended-leg figures include Mary Pickford, Flip, and Punch—all colorful reminders of America's cultural past.*

GLASS ORNAMENTS

Above: *Rare, thin glass figurals, including this angel with paper Dresden wings, the Santa heads, and the moon face were blown in Germany before the British Blockade changed America's Christmas trees forever.*

Greiner, a descendant of one of the founding families, helped to perfect a mirror coating of argentic nitrate, replacing the heavy liquid lead interiors in glass ornaments.

The exteriors were colored in every imaginable hue with a mixture of anilin dyes and gelatin or lacquer. Additional artist's touches included a frosted-milk luster made by using a solution of gelatin and starch, and a brushed effect made by an adhesive gelatin and covering of sparkling silver and gold glass dust. The effect known as "Venetian Dew" was made with a layer of thin glass beading.

From their first appearance, figural ornaments such as gilded glass birds, pinecones, and red-coated *weihnachtsmann* or *Klausmann* (the German Santa Claus) proved popular.

The demand for specific types of ornaments varied by country. Political and fairy-tale figures were popular in Great Britain; comic and humorous figures were sought throughout the United States.

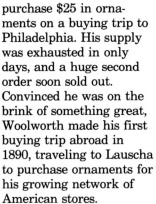

Foxy Grandpa, Happy Hooligan, Mary Pickford, and even Al Jolson found their way onto America's Christmas trees.

In 1890, F. W. Woolworth of 5-and-10-cent-store fame opened the floodgates to the importation of inexpensive ornaments. As owner of a small store in Lancaster, Pennsylvania, he was persuaded to purchase $25 in ornaments on a buying trip to Philadelphia. His supply was exhausted in only days, and a huge second order soon sold out. Convinced he was on the brink of something great, Woolworth made his first buying trip abroad in 1890, traveling to Lauscha to purchase ornaments for his growing network of American stores.

Between World War I and World War II, as many as 15,000 figurals reflecting American, not European, culture were sold—W. C. Fields, the Hindenberg zeppelin, teddy bears, and American Indians, in addition to ever-popular seasonal themes.

Blown baubles declined in 1939, when the British Blockade halted our importation of ornaments from Germany and Czechoslovakia.

Top: *Common yet most desired glass ornaments over the years were birds, messengers of love and harbingers of good things to come.*

Above: *Edibles were the first tree decorations, with fruits and vegetables imitated in glass by German glassblowers in the 1920s.*

WAX AND SEBNITZ ORNAMENTS

Delicate wax angels and intricately worked Sebnitz ornaments are a rare but welcome addition to today's Christmas decor from yesteryear's Victorian yuletide.

Fragile fantasies made from wax rank among the rarest of 19th-century Christmas decorations.

Endearing wax angels heralding the birth of Christ garnered a favored spot on many a Christmas tree. The rarest were manufactured entirely from wax, while the more common consisted of a firm papier-mâché or composition core coated with wax. Clad in detailed dresses and crowned with ringlets of brown and blond wool hair, these angels were completed with finely crafted faces.

From 4 to 14 inches tall, the angels usually featured wings of spun glass, often finished at the end with a tiny gold paper star to which a

Opposite: Sebnitz transportation-themed decorations abound with imagination and creativity.

Right: Wax angels are fragile reminders of the birth of Christ.

thread was attached so that the wings could be properly positioned in the branches. Many Victorian children thought these were indeed the angels of heaven hovering in their tree on Christmas morning.

Dressed in thin gauze material of red, white, or gold, these angels invariably had matching,

multicolored ribbon draped over their shoulders. Some even carried feather tree wreaths, tin and lead trumpets, or flags. The most elegant were outfitted with paper foil wings perched on springs that would shimmer and move with the slightest air currents in the Victorian parlors.

Other early wax decorations included Sebnitz—ornaments that combined wax figures with other materials and were manufactured in Sebnitz, a village at the east end of the Erzgiberge mountains on the Austrian-Hungarian border.

Cottage workers made Sebnitz by covering cotton wool forms with fragile webs made from metallic foil in which small round holes had been stamped by machine. The resulting three-dimensional creations were rich flights of fantasy. Dirigibles, baby beds, an RCA dog sitting by a Victrola, and countless other novelties were created in the late 19th century. Dirigibles and zeppelins were the most popular here, reflecting America's fascination with airships.

There seems to have been no end to the imagination of these cottage workers, whose treasures are discovered anew in the attics and closets of yesteryear.

DRESDEN ORNAMENTS

An array of die-cut elephants, zebras, ostriches, dogs, zeppelins, carriages, and other fanciful figures made by Germany's Dresden artisans are among our most coveted antique Christmas ornaments.

Imagination and fantasy reigned supreme among Germany's Dresden artisans, whose outpouring of tiny animals, vehicles, and musical instruments fed 19th-century America's passion for unusual additions to the Christmas tree.

These Dresden ornaments, so called because they were made in or near Dresden, were crafted as novelties as early as 1850 and reached a zenith in popularity between 1880 and 1910.

Early, flat Dresdens were created from a deeply embossed, heavy paper die cut. The silver- or gold-covered paper was colored with one or two (and sometimes three) transparent lacquers, most often red and green.

Cats, horses, dogs, and rabbits were made, as well as exotic animals such as lions, peacocks, camels, monkeys, and elephants. Deeply embossed shields, stars, bells, and crosses of all sizes also were created.

Human figures, though rare, included mythological warriors and gods, as well as Father Christmases carrying a tree and a toy sack.

Later, as Germans experimented with and perfected their printing presses, they were able to create the most sought after of all today's Christmas collectibles: three-dimensional Dresdens.

These heavily embossed cardboard creations were part of the Luxus-papier industry in Germany from about 1850 to the present. Prior to 1940, real silver and bronze were affixed to the stock before embossing.

Since World War II, only aluminum foil has been used with a lacquer to create the gold color. Age, therefore, is determined by both the appearance and the material used.

Dresden ornaments are two-sided. Although they appeared to be made of metal, the ornaments in fact were made from two or more separately prepared pieces of cardboard, that were deeply embossed. The cardboard was composed of sheets of thin paper with glue spread between them. In the hollow embossing process, each raised area

Above: *Fire engines, locomotives, and balloons perched in Christmas trees as each season brought new novelties to Americans who thirsted for the "best" for their floor-to-ceiling trees.*

Opposite: *Animals (doubling as candy containers), popular in childrens' literature and found only in zoos, were most often purchased by Victorians who savored the unusual.*

DRESDEN ORNAMENTS

in the upper stamp (matrix) corresponded to an identical depression in the bottom stamp (patrix) of the embossing press. The two matching halves were embossed and cut out by huge machines designed for this purpose. The cardboard, when inserted, was slightly damp and elastic, allowing the raised part of the press to push the cardboard deeply into the negative space under great pressure. Next, cottage workers glued the stamped pieces together and smoothed out the seams.

The earliest Dresden ornaments were either in their original plain silver or gold, flashed with a lacquer. But soon they were painted with bright colors for greater realism.

Even though only 2 to 3 inches in size, these charming figures look extremely realistic, especially from a distance. Ships, trains, humans, animals, even household objects such as wash tubs and baby carriages were created in realistic miniatures. The figures were made even more believable with such details as upholstery on sleighs and harnesses and silk-string reins on horses.

Religious forms, first thought to be in rare supply, are quite common. Gold Bethlehem stars, angels, baby Jesus figures, and even fish as symbols of Christ abound.

Originally intended as party favors, table decorations, or candy containers, Dresdens were advertised in wholesale catalogs as early as 1887 by Erlich Brothers, a New York toy wholesaler.

E. Neuman in 1901 also advertised Dresdens as party favors, specifically offering umbrellas, bottles, shoes, purses, books, pots of flowers, and mandolins. Unusual shapes included keys, a bunch of radishes, fruit, a bottle of Benedictine liqueur, and mushrooms. Common animals also found their way into the company's catalog pages. Bulldogs, cats, storks, frogs, fish, pigs, pheasants, foxes, polar bears, bugs, and

Opposite: *Highly detailed and realistic looking, flat and three-dimensional Dresden ornaments float enchantingly among the branches of this paper tree.*

Left: *Simply gilded, painted, and embossed, flat Dresdens are the earliest paper decorations fashioned for trees. Many collectors do not consider the flat cardboard ornaments to be true Dresdens, however.*

Below left: *Dresdens originally were intended as party favors, table decorations, or candy containers. Each of these Dresden musical instruments conceals a compartment for tiny confections and presents.*

lobsters often doubled as hollow candy containers. Even mice dressed in human attire, with open ends for the insertion of candy, were available in the early 1900s.

B. Shackman & Company of New York was still advertising Dresdens immediately prior to World War I. Most of the Dresdens had concealed boxes to be filled with candy.

Available just before the war were upright pianos, violin cases with encased violins, accordions that actually played, and banjos with pictures. Also offered were more elaborate zeppelins, airplanes, mortar boards, cups of chocolate, imitation safety razors, and card tables with cards displayed on top.

Some of the more unique ornaments included doghouses with doors that flew open and silver champagne coolers with bottles packed in cracked ice. Not all of the favors listed were made from paper, however. Tin footballs, imitation leather basketballs and footballs, and even silk balloons also were offered.

Wholesale prices ranged from five to 60 cents each. By the dozen they were even less expensive, 55 cents to $6.80.

Dresdens were manufactured in smaller quantity than other antique ornaments. As a result, fewer are in existence for enjoyment on today's tree. In America, they never reached the great popularity they achieved in Europe because of their relative expense. Originally purchased primarily by wealthier families on the East Coast and in large cities, they were quickly disposed of by families who did not treasure their worth.

Many were discarded when they became tarnished, and were replaced by the cheaper, brighter glass ornaments that caught the fancy of Americans in the period just before World War I.

*S*CRAP ORNAMENTS

From their place on German Christmas cakes in the early 1800s to American trees by the turn of the century, scrap ornaments made of brightly colored paper art and tinsel invoke times past.

Scrap ornaments got their start as Christmas decorations for the table, not for the tree. The earliest were created in Germany from embossed pictures used to decorate Christmas cakes in the early 1800s.

Later, during the post-Civil War era, Americans clamored for these color pictures, made possible by recently invented multi-plate printing processes. The pictures, called scraps because of their use in the then-ubiquitous scrapbooks, eventually found their way to the Christmas tree.

Deeply embossed and subtly colored, scrap ornaments featured pictures of angels, fairy-tale characters, circus animals, small children, Santa Claus and Father Christmas, and Nativity scenes. Among the most coveted were those in which Father Christmas was attired in unusual colors, such as black, brown, and purple.

Tinsel handles and decorative effects were added to the pictures with bits of colored paper and celluloid, which frequently were shredded, scalloped, or cut into thin strips. Most scrap ornaments were finished with pieces of clustered and looped tinsel (*lametta*).

Once their use as tree ornaments caught on,

scraps often were assembled commercially. Bernard Wilmsen, a Philadelphia ornament maker, conceived the idea of combining tinsel with scraps to make a flat, nonbreakable ornament. Easily recognized by a small paper label—"Patented June 7, 1898"—plumes of stutz (tinsel wire) and strips of nitro-cellulose cellophane finished Wilmsen's elaborate decorations.

Extremely popular from the late 1800s to the late 1920s, scrap ornaments only waned in popularity after World War I because of the availability of bright and glittery glass figural ornaments.

Left: Santas were a favorite theme of German printers, who turned out colored paper "scraps" for festive ornaments like this one.

Right: Heavily embossed scrap ornaments from the early 1900s were embellished with tinsel, lametta, and cellophane.

$\mathscr{S}$PUN COTTON ORNAMENTS

One of the folksiest, and rarest, of antique ornaments for the tree is the spun cotton figurine—any of a delightful array of figures upon which, unfortunately, time has not always treaded lightly.

From humble fruit to elaborate St. Nicks, cotton tree decorations made by cottage craftsmen of the Saxon-Thuringian area of Germany from the mid-1870s to the early 1900s fed America's increasing appetite for Christmas ornaments. An endless variety of cotton clowns, farmers, glassblowers, children, and plant sellers were among the tree figures.

The ornaments are made by tightly wrapping glue-moistened cotton around a wire form. When dry, fruits and vegetables were realistically painted. Some were even given fabric leaves for added realism.

The outer surface of some spun cotton ornaments were spread with paste and sprinkled with sparkling glass. Others were fully dressed in paper clothes fancied-up with golden stars, colored flowers, ribbons, and crepe paper aprons.

Unfortunately, old, good-quality pressed cotton ornaments are extremely rare today, due in part to high humidity—a major enemy of cotton. When exposed to moisture, the cotton wads into tight masses or comes apart as the glue gives way, causing mildew and mold to take over.

Left: *Although not as flashy as their fragile glass cousins, three-dimensional cotton-batting Christmas ornaments were a favorite among children.*

Above: *Humble fruits and vegetables fashioned from cotton imitate those first edibles used on trees decades before.*

FEATHER TREES

*No new invention, the artificial tree traces to mid-19th-century
Germany, where wispy feathers from turkeys, geese, ostriches, and
swans re-created the sparsely boughed native German white pine.*

An innovation of the Germans, who relied on the tree as a central symbol of Christmas, the handcrafted imitation Christmas tree dates to the second half of the 19th century.

Many believe the artificial tree with feather boughs arose out of German wholesalers' need to display their Christmas wares year-round, even when it wasn't the season, thus making it hard to justify the cutting of a live tree.

The popularity of feather trees quickly reached America, thanks largely to F. W. Woolworth, who is credited as the first U.S. wholesaler.

Feather tree manufacturing was a cottage industry. The parts for the tree—wire, wood, and berries—were factory produced, then sent to the cottages for wrapping. Turkey and goose feathers were most commonly used, but occasionally ostrich and swan feathers were employed.

Stripping the feathers of their quills after each feather was dyed, the Germans individually wrapped and wired each branch and finished the tip with either a red composition berry or a candle holder.

Pushed into a central wood pole, each branch formed a perfectly shaped, sparse tree reminiscent of the German white pine.

In the 1930s, in an attempt to spur the dwindling sale of green feather trees, the Germans experimented with such vivid colors as variegated green, solid blue, pink, white, and even orange. To further bolster declining sales, electrical sockets were added so trees could be lit.

Earlier trees can be distinguished by round, unadorned turned pots. Square bases appeared in the 1920s, terraced bases just before World War II.

During World War II, feather trees disappeared only to be replaced after the war by wire crepe paper and visca trees.

Above: *Early pre-1900 trees sit in plain, round turned wooden pots. Rarer are those outfitted with candle holders at the tips of selected branches.*

Opposite: *During the late 1920s to 1930s, tree branches were placed a bit closer together to satisfy the desire of Americans for a fuller, more natural, American-appearing tree.*

CANDLE HOLDERS

Candle holders in the 1800s meant far more at Christmas than a mere means to enhancing mood: They were a necessity for illuminating the Christmas tree in the days before electricity.

In the last century, most children's first glimpse of the Christmas tree occurred when the parlor doors were thrown open to reveal a dark, chilled room filled with the flickering glow of candles carefully placed one by one on the fir boughs.

Early candles were thin and long with a heavy wick and were attached to the tree by winding the bottom of a candle around the bough. Later, the blunt end of a needle was heated and pushed into the bottom of the candle so it could be more easily attached to the branch.

After years of experimentation, pinched candle holders were devised. Newspapers chronicled fire upon fire caused by candles, so countless inventors sought to manufacture a "safe" candle holder for the tree.

In 1867, the counterbalance candle holder was created. The earliest and most economical came with a clay or wooden ball at the bottom. A alternative was the V-shaped candle holder, which used two lead counterweights. The most decorative employed soft lead or tin weights in the forms of angels, pinecones, icicles, stars, and Santas.

Glass ornaments often were incorporated with candle holders. Fruit, vegetables, and pinecone blown glass ornaments helped to keep the candles upright. Glass globes were used to hold the candles between 1902 and 1913.

Extension candle holders, an American invention, were patented and sold in 1903. The candle extended from the holder, which was attached to the tree by bending the holder's three tin arms around the branches.

Early candle holders were tin or brass, plain in color, and heavily embossed. They also featured shapes such as fish, Santas, or angels. Other early holders were richly lithographed with Father Christmas, angels on clouds, and children.

Opposite: *Among the most remembered are simple clip-on candle holders pinched onto each branch.*

Above: *Tin lithographed and embossed, these candle holders are among the rarest because they doubled as decorations.*

Right: *Counterweighted holders were designed to prevent the many fires recorded from candles tipping.*

FIGURAL GLASS LIGHTS

*The invention of electricity in the 19th century brought light
to virtually every aspect of American life, including how we decorate
for Christmas.*

Not much more than 100 years ago, during the Christmas of 1882, Thomas Edison's associate, Edward Johnson, became the first person to electrically light a Christmas tree. His homemade strings of 80 small electric lamps marked an indelible change in the way the Christmas tree would be decorated thereafter.

Around 1908, plain tree lamps were replaced in popularity by fancy figural lamps imported from Germany, Austria, and Hungary. Similar to clip-on ornaments, the glass figures had detailed molding, soft shades of paint, and expressive faces. Styles included court jesters and clowns, jack-o'-lanterns and witches, Red Riding Hood and Puss 'n Boots, lions and pigs, Indian braves and maidens, flowers, fruits, nuts, and vegetables. In short supply even when first produced, these figural lights command high prices today.

World War I closed the import market for European goods, but in 1917, Louis Szel went to Japan to start the industry there.

The introduction of milk glass in 1918 soon became a standard for all Szel's Japanese-made lamps. Paint was improved, filaments were standardized to tungsten, and the bases were moved from the bottoms of the lamps to the tops.

Japanese companies produced hundreds of figural varieties, many focusing on current American themes: cars, trains, planes, Santas, nursery rhyme and fairy-tale characters, animals, children, cartoon and comic characters, inanimate objects, and fantasy figures.

Many holiday-themed bulbs were made, including Easter crosses, baby chicks, bunnies, jack-o'-lanterns, witches, and embossed skulls with crossbones on round globes.

The popularity of Japanese milk glass bulbs continued into the 1940s, when war once again changed how we lighted our trees. Americans became fascinated by bubble lights, and figural milk glass never quite regained its popularity.

Like European figurals, Japanese milk glass lights are rare today. Most were discarded when they burned out, and their scarcity means high prices on today's market.

Above left: *Japanese milk glass lights from the 1930s recall fairy tales and comic stories of long ago.*

Opposite: *Early 1900s Austrian and German blown carbon exhaust lamps like these rare examples were quickly replaced by the more inexpensive Japanese manufactured lamps.*

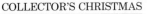

TOYS AND BOOKS

Beginning with the birth of Jesus, Christmas traditionally has been a season for children— and a time for expressing the child at heart. Nothing speaks to this aspect of the holiday better than antique toys and books.

Old Christmas toys and books serve as treasured memories of the past. As playthings that were used, sometimes abused, and often discarded in favor of newer acquisitions, they are understandably somewhat rare today.

The Victorian fascination with parlor games inevitably brought about the manufacturing of many holiday games. These were never produced in huge quantities, however, because they were used only for a short period during the year.

Parker Brothers produced, among countless other games, "The Card Game of Santa Claus"— similar to "Old Maid," except that the player holding the Santa card wins. In 1889, Parker Brothers came out with "The Game of Merry

Left: Wooden puzzles and blocks were covered with richly lithographed Christmas images.

Christmas," a board game. "Christmas Pie" and "The Stocking Game" were also popular.

The first wooden block Christmas puzzles were created by McLoughlin Brothers, which turned six illustrations from *The Night Before Christmas* into the "Santa Claus Cube Puzzle." In 1889, "Around the World with Santa Claus" and "Jolly Santa Picture Cubes" puzzles joined the ranks.

Not all blocks were traditional cubes. Some were flat, like small tiles, with Santa on one side and a letter on the other. These lithograph blocks were so popular that most toy manufacturers offered them. Some of the best were from J. H. Singer and Morton E. Converse & Son, whose blocks were unrivaled for detail, color, and graphic appeal.

Among the finest old toys available today are cast-iron playthings such as a Father Christmas in

101

TOYS AND BOOKS

a toy sleigh pulled by two leaping reindeer.

Clockwork Santas, first produced in 1855 by S. Guntermann, employed motion, with Santa's head rocking back and forth while his eyes moved from side to side.

German-made Lehmann toys, such as Santa riding in mechanical cars, airplanes, and sleighs, were hand-painted, individually assembled, and sometimes even hand-stenciled.

In the years leading up to World War II, a large number of North Pole scenes, complete with tiny lead figures of the entire Santa crew, were imported from Germany.

Most of the first Christmas books were of Christmas plays, but later, many were editions of *The Night before Christmas*. The poem itself appeared in 1823, but it was not published until 1845.

Later, elaborate pop-up books, panoramas such as McLoughlin Brothers' 1870 "Visit of Santa Claus to the Happy Children," and even dioramas such as "Kriss Kringle's Christmas Tableau" (priced at $1.50) were produced.

With their emphasis on Santa and happy promise, no wonder old toys and books are dusted off along with other favorite dreams, come Christmas.

Opposite: *Pre-1900 gifts included Victorian parlor games, roly poly, and a Santa-in-the-box.*

Below: *Lavishly printed and detailed Christmas books chronicled the history of Santa Claus.*

CANDY CONTAINERS

Christmas traditionally is a time for indulging a sweet tooth. It's no surprise, then, that decorative antique holiday candy containers join the ranks of the season's collectibles.

Often given as presents to sweethearts and children on Christmas Day, intricately detailed candy containers were emptied and then saved as keepsakes, thus joining the ranks of today's holiday collectibles. Also saved and recycled as decorations were paper cornucopias originally given to youngsters as Christmas gifts by Sunday school or school teachers.

As early as 1881, Bernard Mayer manufactured and advertised candy boxes and containers. In 1905 Myers and Son advertised multitudes of candy boxes designed solely for the Sunday school market. Lithographed with both secular and religious themes, the boxes appeared in many different forms.

Papier-mâché containers made in Germany and Japan were oval or circular, and featured a cotton child, animal, or Santa figure perched on top. Sometimes placed on skis or snowballs, these figures were finished with wax, bisque, clay, or paper faces. The cardboard boxes were covered with fabric, mica chips, or simply white paint. Invariably, feather branches, tiny glass ornaments, or paper scraps completed the containers.

Paper cornucopias for the Christmas tree were decorated with chromo-lithographs and tinsel sprays with tinsel handles for attachment.

Doing duty in today's homes for the holidays, these candy containers from a bygone time resonate with the sweetest memories.

Left: These candy containers— from Dresden-style fish to cornucopias to table decorations—were all fashioned between 1870 and 1925.

105

*S*TOCKINGS

Hanging at the hearth Christmas Eve, awaiting Santa's arrival to be filled with tasty treats and toys, stockings are a yuletide tradition whose genesis occurs in legend.

Filled with treats, Christmas stockings have delighted generations of children.

Legend attributes the Christmas stocking custom to St. Nicholas, who tossed gold coins down the chimney of three sisters doomed to spinsterhood for want of a dowry. Fortunately, the coins fell directly into the maidens' stockings, hung to dry by the fire, thus starting a lasting tradition.

The earliest literary reference to stockings was made in an 1821 children's book, *A New Year's Present*. In 1837 Robert Walter Weir produced the first painting of St. Nicholas complete with three stockings hung by the fireplace, two laden with toys and one filled with switches.

Many Americans in the 1880s debated whether to hang a stocking or to decorate a tree. Happily, the conflict was resolved by Americans adopting both child-pleasing customs.

Although a plentiful supply of stockings were made throughout the

1800s, few of the early ones have survived because of careless hanging and overstuffing.

Commercially manu-factured stockings soon replaced actual footwear. In the 1880s, lithographed stockings, including do-it-yourself ones made from sheets, were popular. Net took over as the dominant stocking material after World War I.

Above: *Early simple stockings were home-crafted from designs and patterns found in magazines.*

Right: *Many early 1900s stockings such as these were produced from preprinted designs produced on cotton muslin sheets.*

XMAS STOCKING TO BE HUNG UP BY THE CHILDREN FOR SANTA CLAUS

DIRECTIONS

1ST. CUT DOTTED LINE
2ND. TURN TWO PARTS TOGETHER, PRINTED FACE IN.
3RD. TURN INSIDE OUT.
4TH. BUCKLE TO BE SEWED ON TOP OF STOCKING TO HANG BY

PATENTED BY S.H. HONE N.Y. 1886.

Any joy for any other item or any suitableness of fabrication will be prosecuted.

Hang up the Baby's stocking
Be sure you don't forget
The little dimpled Darling
Has ne'er seen Xmas yet!

MERRY CHRISTMAS

CHRISTMAS MEMENTOS

Scrapbooks filled with beautifully decorated holiday images, delicate seasonal china, silver spoons, and fragile fold-up Christmas scenes expand the ranks of holiday collectibles.

Colorful Christmas images printed in Germany fed the scrapbook craze that swept America from the Civil War to the 1880s.

Painstakingly pasted into albums with a homemade flour and water solution, these mementos now serve as treasured reminders of Christmases past.

Even earlier Christmas keepsakes include delicate, holiday-decorated German china chocolate and coffee sets dating to the early 1800s.

To stir their beverages, Christmas revelers had sterling and silver-plated spoons bearing traditional holiday images.

In Victorian times, side tables often featured elaborate fold-out Christmas scenes, fairly expensive even then. To encourage sales, printers attached tiny calendars for year-round use. However, this also guaranteed their disposal at the end of the year. Unfortunately for collectors, many other Christmas mementos also proved fleeting.

Below: Fragile calendars and mechanical pop-up cards from the early 1900s survive as reminders of days long past.

Right: Special Christmas scrapbooks designed exclusively for holiday scraps share a tabletop with delicate German china.

CARDS AND POSTCARDS

Beautifully illustrated Christmas cards from the 19th century were prized even then. Tucked away safely in scrapbooks at first, then later used as tree ornaments, antique cards continue to appeal today.

A century ago, lavish Christmas greeting cards were saved in scrapbooks and later used as decorations for the tree.

Although the precise origins aren't known, some Christmas historians trace holiday greeting cards to 18th-century schoolboys, who composed intricate letters to their parents to show their progress in penmanship. Written on hand-decorated paper, these letters were so enjoyed by parents that the boys began including them as part of their Christmas gifts to family.

The first commercial Christmas card was introduced in December 1843 by John Horsley, who made the card at the request of his friend Sir Henry Cole. A thousand copies (12 of which still remain) were lithographed and sold in London. Two panels that

Left: *An array of early 1900s German printed postcards illustrates Santa and his many legends brought to life and preserved in history.*

Above: *This transparency card reveals Father Christmas when held up to the light. Such cards also illustrate Christmas customs in toys, tree decorations, and childrens' attire.*

illustrated feeding the hungry and clothing the naked so aroused public anger that the cards were withdrawn and the entire

venture was termed a flop. Later, however, the practice of sending Christmas cards grew, even spreading to the continent.

111

CARDS AND POSTCARDS

Louis Prang, a German lithographer who moved to the United States in 1850, popularized greeting cards. Introducing Christmas cards to America in 1875, he immediately became successful because of his color printing process, which employed up to 20 plates.

Prang's early cards followed the British vogue of the day—humor, flowers, animals, elegant ladies, children, and scenes often unrelated to Christmas.

In fact, many collectors often mistake Prang's Christmas cards for Valentines because they were so adorned with ribbons, lace, and flowers. Prang quit the card business in the 1890s in disgust, when the penny postcard craze swept the United States.

Publisher Charles Goodall & Son entered the business by way of another kind of card: the one used for visiting. At the time, middle and upper-class Americans made formal calls on friends, customarily leaving a visiting card. Goodall expanded upon this idea by designing special cards for holiday visits. These early cards typically were ornate and usually in the form of a bouquet or basket of flowers. Ribbons or tabs could be pulled up or down from the card to open the flowers and reveal messages of health, happiness, and goodwill. Some had ribbons or cords so they could be hung; others were meant to be preserved in ornate

Above: *This card from the late 1800s reveals not only candles but the home-crafted tree stand into which the tree was placed* and camouflaged with moss.
Top left: *Unlike this one, early Christmas cards often featured scenes unrelated to the holiday.*

Top right: *Because of the sentimental verse and graphics, 1880s Christmas cards frequently were mistaken for valentines.*

frames. From Christmas visiting cards, it was a short step for Goodall to make cards much like those we send today.

Children's book illustrator Kate Greenaway also contributed to the design of greeting cards; hers are considered masterpieces of greeting card art.

The 1893 World's Columbian Exposition in Chicago led to production of the modern card. For this event, Charles Goldsmith persuaded the United States Post Office to license him to print illustrated souvenir cards of the fair on government postals (which had been introduced earlier, in 1873).

The modern greeting card industry began in the early 1900s with the birth of such companies as Hallmark Cards (then Hall Brothers, Inc.), Rust Craft, Buzza, and American Greetings.

Christmas has been incorporated on postcards from the very beginning. By 1907, German, British, and American postcards were being devoured by an enthusiastic public.

Card designs and their use of Christmas symbols have changed over the years. Mistletoe and holly were used on the earliest cards; St. Nicholas made his first appearance in the 1850s. Silk fringe borders became the fad in the 1880s, but it took until the late 1890s for Christmas trees to appear on cards. The first religious cards appeared in the 1890s, and poinsettias were virtually unknown until the early 1900s.

The rarest of Santa cards include hold-to-light, transparency, silk, mechanical, and full European figured cards. The hold-to-lights are especially valued by collectors for their

composition—multilayers of cardboard, with the top layer containing the picture cut out at strategic points that correspond to a Santa figure or scene. Backing these cuts is translucent paper that permits a light source to illuminate the scene. The hold-to-lights have been found with postmarks as early as 1899. It is believed that as many as 200 different cards of this type were produced.

Transparency postcards are similar to hold-to-light cards in that they contain a blank space in a design that otherwise fills the front of the card. A scene of children decorating a tree will reveal the figure of Father Christmas observing the scene if the card is held up to bright light. These cards are extremely scarce and are priced accordingly.

Early cards had pieces of silk fabric glued to

Above: *This 1880s silk fringed card with birds, holly, and a serene winter setting is typical of the period.*

them, while countless others had fringes of silk around the entire card. Most often Santa's robes, and occasionally the clothes of children and hides of animals, were covered with different color silks. The rarest colors for Santa's robe were brown, white, purple, green, and blue; the most common color was red.

Mechanical postcards with moving parts are also extremely desirable. On some cards, Santa's facial expression would change when a tab in the top of the card was pulled. Other cards featured eyes that opened and closed, arms that moved, and even a Santa whose pack of toys shifted.

FESTIVE FEASTING

For centuries, good cooks have shared the joys of the season through their culinary artistry, creating holiday repasts fit for royalty.

REGIONAL FEASTS

Though a well-dressed turkey and a plump mince pie are placed on holiday tables from coast to coast, regionality makes itself—and its flavors—known.

Today's mobile population has created an American diet that is seemingly homogeneous. Yet regional flavors still distinguish one area of the country from another.

YANKEE COOKING

The fare of the northeastern states continues to reflect the creativity with which early settlers incorporated new, unfamiliar ingredients into recipes they brought with them from the old country.

Left: A menu from the Pacific Northwest celebrates nature's bounty on land and sea. Nut-filled sweets, such as the Black Walnut Cake pictured here (see recipe, page 119), are a regional favorite.

Previous pages: A traditional Yankee feast included roast beef, Yorkshire pudding, and steamed sweet potatoes.

When they first landed on American shores, the settlers discovered wild turkeys, pumpkins, sweet potatoes, corn, and cranberries; today, the meal that defines the holidays for most of America includes these native foods. Consider the menu: roast turkey, cornbread stuffing, sweet potato casserole, cranberry sauce, and pumpkin pie.

An alternative Yankee Christmas menu shows the influence of English ancestry here: oyster stew, roast beef with Yorkshire pudding, and plum pudding.

MIDWEST MENUS

In the Midwest, many a good cook lays upon the table a fine baked ham, turkey with oyster dressing, scalloped corn, sweet potatoes baked with nuts and brown sugar, yeast rolls, and cranberries, then makes

REGIONAL FEASTS

the menu uniquely midwestern with foods—particularly breads, cakes, and cookies—reflecting a Scandinavian heritage. Among these foods are coarse, heavy rye breads; *julekake* (a sweet yeast bread); rich, spicy cookies; and the potato-based flatbread called *lefse*.

SOUTHERN SEASONINGS

In the South, a typical feast might begin with a creamy bisque. Ham is almost always served next, but unlike the hams eaten in other parts of the country, Southern hams (including Smithfield and Virginia cures), are dry, salty, and strong in flavor. They're sliced paper thin, and the slivers are eaten with crackerlike beaten biscuits.

The holidays are testimony to the bounty of southern hospitality. A southern host or hostess presents a groaning board, with angel biscuits and butter, whole-wheat biscuits and cream gravy, green beans and bacon, collards, stewed tomatoes, sweet potatoes, jam cake, chess pie, and cookies.

CAJUN COOKING

Southern Louisiana is distinct from other southern states, with flavors all its own. This is Cajun country: Reflected here is the cooking of the Choctaw and Chickasaw Indians and that of the area's French, Spanish, and Jamaican settlers.

Cajun cooking, based on seafood, sausages, rice, and peppers, is full of fire

and spice. Jambalaya, for example—one of the most distinctive Cajun specialties—is made of rice, meat or poultry, tomatoes, and hot peppers.

Dirty rice is a grayish dressing that *does* look dirty, thanks to its combination of rice, sweet green peppers, and chicken giblets. *Maque choux,* an Indian specialty, is a gruellike corn stew that today often is prepared outdoors over an open fire, just as it was when the land was wild.

A Cajun meal is a generous one, and the holidays are an excuse to bring out favorite recipes: spicy potato salads, black-eyed peas and bacon, deep-fried sweet potatoes, and long loaves of French bread with homemade preserves. Daunting wedges of pecan pie or meringue-topped bread pudding—or both—ensure that no one will leave a Cajun cook's holiday table less than sated.

SPICE OF THE SOUTHWEST

In the Southwest, culinary artistry is as colorful as the local sunsets. Here there is a nearly spiritual reverence for food, inspired by the Native American beliefs that every morsel—grain or fruit or beast—was a gift from the gods, mother earth and father sun.

Preparing a meal and dining together are celebrations in themselves in the Southwest, and a holiday feast is an important ritual, indeed.

Corn is prominent in this region's cooking, for it is the most important food in the Indian culture. The Pueblos and Navajos have more than 250 ways to prepare corn, and use it in mush, breads, stews, cookies, and cakes.

Corn is used in tamales, which are served on almost any feast day. Tamales are made with a dough of fine cornmeal that's filled with a savory meat mixture or a sugary fruit one, then wrapped in corn husks and steamed.

Traditionally, *posole*—a hearty stew of hominy (fat corn kernels), green chile, and pork—is simmered much of the day before Christmas, then served for supper at midnight.

On Christmas day, there might be tacos with shredded pork, beans, rice, pumpkin stew, breads baked of blue cornmeal, corn pudding, pralines, and pine nut cookies.

NORTHWEST BOUNTY

The Pacific Northwest is replete with the raw ingredients of its fresh and flavorful cuisine. Clams, crab, salmon, and other fish come from the water; lamb, beef, dairy cattle, and chicken come from the land. The fertile soil in this region yields wild mushrooms, black walnuts, hazelnuts, apples, plums, cherries, legumes, and vegetables in abundance.

Smoked or poached salmon is often the appetizer for festive meals; an assortment of salads made with dried beans and pickled vegetables might accompany an entrée of roast beef or chicken. Among the sweets are nut-filled cookies and cakes, and pies and tarts piled high with locally grown apples, pears, or wild berries.

The following recipes provide a sampling of regional flavors.

SOUTHERN BEATEN BISCUITS

2 cups all-purpose flour
1 teaspoon sugar
¼ teaspoon baking powder
⅛ teaspoon cream of tartar
¼ cup lard
 Very thinly sliced country ham

■ Combine flour, sugar, baking powder, cream of tartar, and ½ teaspoon *salt*. Cut in lard till mixture resembles coarse crumbs. Make a well in the center. Add ¾ cup *ice water* all at once; stir well. If necessary, stir in enough additional ice water to make a stiff dough.

■ Turn out onto a lightly floured surface. Beat vigorously with the flat side of a wooden or metal mallet for 15 minutes, turning and folding dough constantly. Roll or pat to ¼-inch thickness. Cut with a floured 2-inch biscuit cutter. Place on an ungreased baking sheet. Prick biscuit tops several times with the tines of a fork.

■ Bake in a 400° oven about 20 minutes or till crisp (biscuits will be very light in color). Split biscuits; serve with sliced ham. Makes 24.

SOUTHWEST TAMALES

36 large dried corn husks
 3 to 3½ pounds pork shoulder roast
 2 cloves garlic, minced
¼ cup shortening
1½ teaspoons chili powder
¾ teaspoon ground cumin
⅛ teaspoon dried oregano, crushed
¼ cup Mexican-style chili sauce
½ teaspoon crushed red pepper
½ teaspoon bottled hot pepper sauce
 4 cups Masa Harina tortilla flour

■ Soak corn husks in hot water for 2 hours or till very tender. In a Dutch oven, cover pork with water; bring to boiling. Simmer, covered, for 2 hours. Drain, reserving broth. Cut up meat; discard fat and bone. Return meat to pan with 2 cups reserved broth. Simmer, covered, about 30 minutes. Drain, reserving broth; stir chili powder, cumin, and oregano into broth.

■ Shred pork. Brown pork and garlic in shortening. Add broth, chili sauce, red pepper, pepper sauce, and ½ teaspoon *salt*. Simmer, covered, for 30 minutes. Uncover; simmer 15 minutes. Combine flour and 1 teaspoon *salt*. Add water to broth to equal 3 cups; stir into mixture. For each tamale, spread 1 husk out flat; spread 1 rounded tablespoon of dough to within 1 inch of the edges. Top with 1 rounded tablespoon of filling. Fold long edge of husk over filling so it overlaps dough about ½ inch; roll up jelly-roll style. Fold 1 end; tie with string.

■ Place tamales, open side up, in a steamer basket in a large Dutch oven. Add water to just below basket level; bring to boiling. Cover; steam for 1 hour or till tamales pull away from wrappers. Add water to pan as necessary. Remove corn husks from tamales to serve. Makes 36.

NORTHWEST BLACK WALNUT CAKE

1 cup butter or margarine
4 cups sifted powdered sugar
1 teaspoon vanilla
4 egg yolks
2¾ cups all-purpose flour
2½ teaspoons baking powder
½ teaspoon ground cinnamon
1½ cups milk
1 cup chopped black walnuts
4 egg whites
1 8-ounce package cream cheese, softened
1 cup butter
1½ teaspoons vanilla
4½ to 4¾ cups sifted powdered sugar

■ Grease and lightly flour three 8x1½-inch round baking pans. Set aside. In a large mixer bowl beat 1 cup butter with an electric mixer on high speed for 30 seconds. On low speed gradually beat in 2 cups powdered sugar and 1 teaspoon vanilla. Continue beating on high speed till light and fluffy. Add egg yolks, one at a time, beating till thoroughly combined after each addition.

■ Stir together flour, 2 cups powdered sugar, baking powder, cinnamon, and ¼ teaspoon *salt*. Add flour mixture and milk alternately to butter mixture, beating well after each addition. Stir in walnuts.

■ In a small mixer bowl with clean beaters beat egg whites on high speed till stiff peaks form. Gently fold beaten egg whites into the creamed mixture. Divide batter evenly among the 3 baking pans. Bake in a 350° oven about 35 minutes. Cool in pans for 10 minutes on wire racks. Remove from pans; cool completely on racks.

■ For frosting, beat together the cream cheese, 1 cup butter, and 1½ teaspoons vanilla with an electric mixer till light and fluffy. Gradually add the 4½ to 4¾ cups powdered sugar, beating till smooth and creamy. Spread between layers of cake; frost top and sides. Store cake in the refrigerator. Makes 12 servings.

MINCEMEAT

"He that discovered the new star in Cassiopeia deserves not half so much to be remembered as he that first married meat and raisins," an early English writer pronounced in praise of mincemeat. Kings and commoners alike have relished this exotic sweet and meaty mixture for more than 700 years.

Mincemeat pies have filled the winter air with their spicy scent for centuries, their sweet meat and fruit fillings baking in the kitchens of kings' castles, crofters' cottages, and log cabins in the American West. So lengthy is the seasonal association that mincemeat virtually has come to taste like Christmas, evoking all of the day's sensory splendors.

EASTERN ORIGINS

The origins of mincemeat—a rich mixture of meat, suet, fruit, and spices—are obscure, but date back to the Crusades, when the knights brought back exotic spices from the East.

Opposite: *Mincemeat fills a variety of holiday baked goods, including Mincemeat-Cherry Pie (see recipe, page 125).*

The most famous result of this melding of ingredients—the mince pie—may have been born when a daring cook, preparing for a holiday feast, stirred these unfamiliar spices with minced meat, dried fruits, lemon peel and juice, and sweetening, then baked the mixture in a rectangular crust. The Christmas association was strengthened by lore that likened the shape of the pie to Christ's manger, and its spices to the exotic offerings of the Wise Men.

Now, as we bring forth the grand finale to Christmas dinner, we can rejoice with Washington Irving, who wrote of his pie, "I was happy to find my old friend, mince pie, in the retinue of the feast . . . I greeted him with all the warmth wherewith we usually greet an old and very genteel acquaintance."

TRADITIONAL MINCEMEAT

1½ pounds lean beef rump, neck, or chuck, cubed
½ pound suet, finely chopped
4 pounds firm, tart apples, peeled, cored, and finely chopped
1 15-ounce package dark raisins
1 15-ounce package golden raisins
1 10-ounce package currants
⅔ cup diced citron
⅔ cup diced candied fruit
2 cups sugar
½ cup molasses
4 teaspoons ground cinnamon
2 teaspoons salt
1½ teaspoons ground nutmeg
1½ teaspoons ground mace
¼ teaspoon pepper
3 cups cider
2 cups sherry
1 cup brandy

■ In a medium saucepan cover beef with water. Boil 1½ hours or till tender. Cool. In a blender or food processor finely chop meat.

■ In a large kettle combine meat with suet, apples, dried and candied fruits, sugar, molasses, spices, and cider. Bring to boiling, stirring occasionally. Add sherry and brandy. Simmer for 30 minutes, stirring often. If mixture becomes too thick, add more cider.

■ To freeze: Place 1- or 2-cup portions in moisture- and vaporproof containers. Seal, label, and freeze. Makes 10 pints.

ℋOLIDAY BAKING

A firing of the hearth and its aromatic results are intrinsic to the holidays, simple reminders of what's good and generous in all of us.

American bakers draw from a rich heritage when they bake up holiday foods whose histories are centuries old.

Since the beginning of culinary experimentation, baked goods have evolved as symbols of the very essence of home. In this country, early cooks baked recipes handed down for generations, and the foods helped keep the past alive in a new land.

These recipes that provided sustenance for both body and soul became particularly significant during the winter holidays.

CHRISTMAS BREADS

Nearly every country has a Christmas bread: Czechoslovakia has its *Vánočka* (Christmas) braid, a sweet loaf studded with raisins and almonds; Germany has its similar stollen. In Sweden, bakers prepare *Saffransbröd*, a saffron bread served for breakfast on Santa Lucia Day on December 13.

Above: *Swedish Kringler consists of a cream-puff-like dough spread over a rich pastry, then topped with a powdered sugar glaze and, sometimes, drizzled with chocolate. (See recipe, page 124.)*

Right: *Currant Scones, served with Strawberry Butter, and Fruit Tarts (see recipes, page 125) transform a simple afternoon tea into an extraordinary event.*

HOLIDAY BAKING

In Italy, bakers prepare *panettone*, a tall, cylindrical loaf made with dried fruits and nuts, and a sweet bread pudding. Mexican celebrants prepare Three King's Cake for Epiphany.

Cookies are a very important part of holiday celebrations, too. Filling Christmas cookie jars are such favorites as Norwegian butter cookies, Swedish spice cookies, Scandinavian *sandbakelser* (sand tarts) and *krumkake*, Italian pizzelles, Scottish shortbread, and German *lebkuchen*.

SWEDISH KRINGLER
(pictured on page 122)

    1 cup butter
    2 cups all-purpose flour
    3 eggs
    ½ teaspoon almond extract
    1 cup sifted powdered sugar
    1 tablespoon butter, softened
    ¼ teaspoon almond extract
    1 to 2 tablespoons whipping cream or milk
    ½ of a 4-ounce bar German sweet cooking
          chocolate
    1 tablespoon butter

■ Cut ½ cup butter into 1 cup flour till pieces are the size of small peas. Sprinkle with 1 tablespoon water; toss with a fork till all is moist. Form into a ball; divide in half. On a cookie sheet pat each half into a 12x3-inch strip. Heat ½ cup butter and 1 cup water to boiling. Remove from heat.

■ Stir in 1 cup flour till smooth. Cool for 15 minutes. Add eggs one at a time, beating after each addition. Stir in ½ teaspoon almond extract. Spread half of the mixture over each pastry strip. Bake at 350° for 55 to 60 minutes or till golden. Cool on a wire rack.

■ For glaze, combine powdered sugar, 1 tablespoon butter, and ¼ teaspoon almond extract. Stir in enough cream to make of spreading consistency. Drizzle over pastries. Melt chocolate and 1 tablespoon butter; drizzle over pastries. Makes 2.

PEAR TART
(pictured on pages 126–127)

    1 cup all-purpose flour
    ½ cup toasted, finely chopped almonds
    ¼ cup sugar
    ¼ cup butter or margarine
    1 egg, beaten
    4 pears, peeled and sliced (4 cups)
    1 teaspoon finely shredded lemon peel
    3 tablespoons lemon juice
    2 eggs
    ¾ cup whipping cream
    ⅓ cup sugar
    ½ teaspoon vanilla
    ¼ teaspoon ground nutmeg

■ Combine the flour, almonds, and ¼ cup sugar. Cut in butter till mixture resembles coarse crumbs. Stir in 1 egg till mixture forms a ball.

■ Pat over bottom and up sides of a greased 10-inch tart pan. Bake in a 425° oven for 10 minutes. Remove from oven; reduce oven temperature to 375°.

■ Toss pear slices with lemon juice; arrange in the tart shell. In a mixing bowl combine the eggs, whipping cream, ⅓ cup sugar, lemon peel, vanilla, and nutmeg; stir till well mixed. Pour over pears.

■ Bake in a 375° oven for 35 to 40 minutes or till set. Cool on a wire rack. Serves 12.

MINCEMEAT-CHERRY PIE
(pictured on page 120)

   Pastry for 2-crust 9-inch pie
1 21-ounce can cherry pie filling
1 cup Traditional Mincemeat (see recipe, page
      121)
¼ cup chopped walnuts
¼ cup orange marmalade
2 teaspoons all-purpose flour

■ Prepare and roll out pastry. Line a 9-inch pie
plate with half of the pastry; trim pastry to ½
inch beyond edge of pie plate.

■ Combine pie filling, mincemeat, nuts,
marmalade, and flour. Spoon into pastry-lined pie
plate. Cut remaining pastry into ½-inch strips.
Weave strips over filling to make lattice. Fold
bottom pastry over lattice strips; seal and flute
edge. Cover edge with foil to prevent
overbrowning. Bake in a 375° oven for 20
minutes. Remove foil; bake for 20 to 25 minutes
more. Makes 8 servings.

CRANBERRY TART
(pictured on pages 126–127)

1   cup all-purpose flour
⅓   cup ground walnuts
¼   cup sugar
¼   cup butter
1   egg, beaten
12   ounces fresh or frozen cranberries (3 cups)
¼   cup orange juice
1½   cups sugar
3   tablespoons cornstarch
⅓   cup walnut halves

■ Combine flour, ground walnuts, sugar, and ¼
teaspoon salt. Cut in butter till mixture resembles
small peas. Add egg. Toss till all is moist, adding
1 tablespoon water, if necessary.

■ Form into a ball; press evenly onto bottom and
up sides of a 10-inch tart pan. Bake at 400° for 10
minutes.

■ Combine cranberries, juice, and ⅓ cup water.
Cook and stir till cranberries pop. Combine sugar
and cornstarch; stir into cranberry mixture. Cook
and stir till thickened and bubbly.

■ Spread in tart shell. Arrange walnut halves on
top. Bake in a 375° oven about 25 minutes. Makes
12 servings.

MINCEMEAT OR FRUIT TARTS
(pictured on pages 122–123 and 133)

2   cups all-purpose flour
1   teaspoon salt
⅔   cup shortening
6   to 7 tablespoons cold water
2½   cups prepared mincemeat or chunk-style apple
        sauce, or 1 pint fresh strawberries, hulled
½   cup apple jelly or currant jelly

■ In a medium bowl stir together the flour and
the salt. Cut in the shortening till pieces are the
size of small peas. Sprinkle 1 tablespoon of the
cold water over part of the mixture; gently toss
with a fork. Push to side of bowl. Repeat till all is
moistened. Form the dough into a ball.

■ Using about ¼ cup mixture for each tart shell,
press dough into 2-inch tart pans to make 20
shells. Place shells on a baking sheet. Bake in a
450° oven for 8 to 10 minutes or till shells are
golden. Cool slightly; carefully remove from pans.
Cool shells completely on wire rack before filling.

■ Spoon about 2 tablespoons mincemeat or apple
sauce into each shell, or fill shells with halved,
sliced, or whole strawberries. In a small saucepan
over low heat, melt the jelly. Brush the jelly
lightly over filling in shells. Makes 20 tarts.

CURRANT SCONES
WITH STRAWBERRY BUTTER
(pictured on page 123)

2   cups all-purpose flour
2   tablespoons sugar
1   tablespoon baking powder
1   teaspoon finely shredded orange peel
¼   teaspoon salt
½   cup butter or margarine
½   cup currants
½   cup whipping cream
1   10-ounce package frozen strawberries, thawed
1   cup butter, softened
1   cup sifted powdered sugar

■ Combine flour, sugar, baking powder, orange
peel, and salt. Cut in butter till mixture
resembles coarse crumbs. Add currants; stir in
cream till dough clings together. Pat dough into
an 8-inch circle. Cut into 12 wedges, or cut with a
cookie cutter. Bake on an ungreased baking sheet
in a 450° oven for 12 to 15 minutes or till golden.

■ In a blender container combine strawberries, 1
cup butter, and powdered sugar. Cover and blend
till smooth. Serve with scones. Makes 12 scones.

HOLIDAY BAKING

LATTICE-TOP APPLE PIE

Pastry for double-crust pie
6   cups peeled, thinly sliced cooking apples
2   tablespoons apple brandy
2   tablespoons minced candied ginger
1   cup sugar
3   tablespoons all-purpose flour
½   teaspoon each ground cinnamon and nutmeg
2   tablespoons butter or margarine

■ Prepare and roll out pastry. Line a 9-inch pie plate with half of pastry; trim to edge of plate. Combine apples, brandy, and ginger. Combine sugar, flour, cinnamon, and nutmeg. Toss with apple mixture. Spoon into plate; dot butter on top.

■ Roll out remaining pastry; top pie with lattice crust. Trim and flute edge. Cover edge with foil. Bake at 375° for 25 minutes; remove foil. Bake 20 to 25 minutes more. Cool on wire rack. Serves 8.

LEMON MERINGUE PIE

Pastry for single-crust pie
1½ cups sugar
3   tablespoons cornstarch
3   tablespoons all-purpose flour
1½ cups water
4   egg yolks
2   tablespoons butter or margarine
1   tablespoon finely shredded lemon peel
⅓   cup lemon juice
6   egg whites
1   teaspoon vanilla
½   teaspoon cream of tartar
¾   cup sugar

■ Prepare and roll out pastry. Line a 9-inch pie plate; trim and flute edge. Prick pastry. Bake at 450° for 10 to 12 minutes or till golden. In a saucepan combine sugar, cornstarch, flour, and dash *salt*. Gradually stir in water. Cook and stir over medium-high heat till thickened and bubbly; cook and stir 2 minutes more. Remove from heat.

■ Beat yolks; stir in 1 cup hot mixture. Return to pan; bring to gentle boil. Cook and stir 2 minutes. Remove from heat. Stir in butter and peel. Gradually stir in lemon juice. Pour into pastry shell.

■ For meringue, in bowl beat egg whites, vanilla, and tartar till soft peaks form. Gradually add ¾ cup sugar, beating till stiff peaks form. Spread over pie, sealing to edge. Bake at 325° for 15 to 18 minutes or till golden. Cool on rack. Serves 8.

Right: *A holiday dessert buffet offers a selection of pies and tarts (see recipes, pages 124-125 and above).*

PLUM PUDDING

How round it is! A kiss is round, the horizon is round, the earth is round, the moon is round, the sun and stars and all the host of heaven are round. So is plum pudding.—The London Illustrated Times, 1848

No writer has described so accurately or so charmingly the Christmas plum pudding as Charles Dickens did in *A Christmas Carol*. Recounting the Cratchit family's Christmas dinner and its beautiful plum pudding, Dickens wrote: "In half a minute Mrs. Cratchit entered—flushed, but smiling proudly—with the pudding, like a speckled cannon-ball, so hard and firm, blazing in half of half-a-quarter of ignited brandy, and bedight with Christmas holly stuck into the top. Oh, a wonderful pudding!"

EARLY SUPERSTITIONS

In England, a host of beliefs and superstitions grew up around the making and serving of Christmas pudding.

The Collect read in the Church of England on the last Sunday before Advent, for example, begins with the words,

Opposite: Plum Pudding, a dense, rich steamed cake, is served with Hard Sauce, lemon sauce, or cream.

"Stir up we beseech Thee . . . ." This phrase was regarded as an admonition to start the plum pudding at once.

And so it was. Each member of the family, eyes closed, took a turn stirring the pudding and making a wish.

GOOD OMENS

As the batter was mixed, a ring, a coin, a thimble, and a button (each wrapped in paper so they could be seen and not swallowed) were added. It was said that whoever found the ring in his or her serving would be married in the coming year. The coin predicted wealth, the thimble, spinsterhood, and the button, bachelorhood.

In the 1800s, puddings were cooked long and slow so that the suet used for shortening would be melted and dispersed throughout the pudding. It was said that a plum pudding took three days to cook and three weeks to ripen. Some families, in fact, cooked the pudding one year, but did not eat it until the next.

PLUM PUDDING

    3 slices bread, torn into pieces
    1 5⅓-ounce can evaporated milk
    2 ounces beef suet, ground
   ¾ cup packed brown sugar
    1 beaten egg
   ¼ cup orange juice
   ½ teaspoon vanilla
 1½ cups raisins
   ¾ cup snipped pitted dates
   ½ cup diced mixed candied fruits and peels
   ⅓ cup chopped walnuts
   ¾ cup all-purpose flour
 1½ teaspoons ground cinnamon
   ¾ cup all-purpose flour
 1½ teaspoons ground cinnamon
   ¾ teaspoon baking soda
   ¾ teaspoon each *ground cloves and ground mace*
        Hard Sauce

■ In a large bowl soak bread in evaporated milk about 3 minutes; beat lightly to break up. Stir in suet, sugar, egg, juice, and vanilla. Add raisins, dates, fruits and peels, and nuts. Combine flour, cinnamon, soda, cloves, mace, and ¼ teaspoon *salt*. Add to fruit mixture; stir till combined.

■ Pour into a well-greased 6½-cup tower mold. Cover with foil, pressing foil tightly against rim of the mold. Place on a rack in a deep kettle; add boiling water to a depth of 1 inch. Cover kettle; boil gently for 4 hours, adding more boiling water, if necessary. Cool for 10 minutes; unmold. Serve warm with hard sauce. Serves 8.

Hard Sauce: Beat together ½ cup *butter*, 1 cup *powdered sugar*, 2 tablespoons *whipping cream*, ½ teaspoon *lemon peel*, and ½ teaspoon *vanilla*. Beat in 1 cup more *powdered sugar* till smooth.

CHRISTMAS CANDIES

*It is not only for children that generations
of confectionery artists have created their
festive masterpieces.*

Candies have been associated with holiday celebrations since confectioners began experimenting with sugar and chocolate centuries ago. Although the confectioner's craft is an ephemeral one—for sugar sculptures dissolve and chocolate masterpieces melt—history reveals a great creativity with the art. Nineteenth-century drawings and descriptions indicate an adroit hand and a fascination with shaping sugar.

CANDY ARTISTRY

As with other culinary arts, candymaking has also been taught by masters in one generation to apprentices in the next.

Each new confectionery artist must learn the effects of temperature and humidity on chocolate,

and know how sugar changes as it is cooked. The artist must be able to combine ingredients in precise proportions to make such things as fudge, marzipan, and butterscotch. Ultimately, the true confectionery artist must have a passion to re-create—for each new masterpiece is all too quickly consumed.

VICTORIAN APPETITES

In this country, the candy industry grew rapidly throughout the 1800s, driven by an insatiable Victorian appetite for sweets. Penny candies first appeared in stores in the mid-1800s. With a penny in hand, a child could buy licorice whips, cinnamon drops, sourballs, and Clear Toys— hard candies to hang on Christmas trees for good girls and boys.

Today, the holidays inspire dreams of sugarplums and an indulgence in sweets—and reveries in the nostalgia they evoke.

*Left: A dark chocolate box,
wrapped and tied with a milk
chocolate ribbon, holds dozens
of creamy truffles.*

131

HOLIDAY TEAS

For meals both simple and extravagant, the tea table long has been a treasured symbol of refinement in American dining.

The tradition of teatime is a long and cherished one. In Victorian America, the final meal on any festive day often was a tea, especially during the holiday season. It was in December when Americans went calling on one another with the most fervor and attention, and teas were served both late afternoons and evenings.

TEATIME AS ART

Teatime entertaining was elevated to an art form; the festive spirit inherent in the Christmas season fueled the love of the art. Victorian women took great pride in the social skills they could display at teatime. They set tables with their finest snowy linens, sterling flatware, and precious china, and made dazzling centerpieces with flowers, candles, and sweets.

HOLIDAY REPASTS

On Christmas day, even though an enormous feast had been served midday,

teatime was not to be missed. A typical menu included tea with cream, brown bread with butter and marmalade, comb honey, dainty sandwiches, meats left over from the earlier meal—ham, shaved beef, chicken, and tongue—cookies and biscuits, berries, frosted cake, sponge cake, dark fruit cake, and custard. This festive tea might be set out for an intimate gathering of family and kin, or for a large group of friends.

Though teas became less elaborate after the turn of the century, hostesses continued to offer equally satisfying though simpler forms of sustenance at teatime, and still do so today.

Opposite: *A fireside table is set for an English-inspired high tea. Though the menu is less elaborate than that typical of a 19th-century tea, it still provides a variety of savories, including Salmon Paté Tea Sandwiches (see recipe, above) and Mincemeat and Fruit Tarts (see recipe, page 125).*

SALMON PÂTÉ TEA SANDWICHES

  8 *ounces cold poached salmon or smoked salmon*
  8 *ounces unsalted butter*
  3 *small green onions, minced*
     Thinly sliced whole wheat bread

■ In a food processor combine salmon and butter; process till smooth. Add green onions; process till combined. Spread bread thinly with *softened butter;* spread with salmon mixture. Cut bread into quarters; top with *fresh basil leaves.* Makes about 2 cups spread.

GINGERSNAPS

2¼ *cups all-purpose flour*
  2 *teaspoons baking soda*
  1 *teaspoon each ground ginger, ground cinnamon, and ground cloves*
 ¼ *teaspoon salt*
  1 *cup packed brown sugar*
 ¾ *cup shortening or cooking oil*
 ¼ *cup molasses*
  1 *egg*

■ Stir together the flour, baking soda, ginger, cinnamon, cloves, and salt. In a large mixer bowl combine the brown sugar, shortening, molasses, and egg. Beat well. Add flour mixture and beat till well mixed. Shape dough into 1-inch balls.

■ Place 2 inches apart on an ungreased cookie sheet. Bake in a 375° oven about 10 minutes or till done. Remove cookies from cookie sheet; cool on wire racks. Makes about 48.

DRINK YE AND BE MERRY

During the shortened days of winter, when the weather seems cruel and without end, a toast by the fire can soothe the soul as well as warm the blood.

In early America, saints and sinners—rich and poor alike—considered the local tavern a second home. The pub provided the pulse of political and social life, the place where everyone could exchange news and gossip and quaff quantities of favorite beverages: beer, ale, hard cider, and rum.

COLONIAL SPIRITS

Soon after the colonists' arrival in Plymouth, breweries were established to keep the pubs well stocked, and kegs of kill-devil or rum rolled in on ships from the West Indies.

With these spirits, tavern keepers concocted amazing libations. A favorite was the flip, made of heated beer or ale, molasses, spices, a dash of rum, and eggs.

Another, more elegant drink was syllabub. It's

Opposite: Syllabub, an eggnoglike drink, was served to the ladies and even to the children in Elizabethan days.

similar to eggnog, but not as rich. Made with wine, sherry, or cider instead of stronger spirits, it was considered a suitable beverage for ladies, and even children were permitted to have syllabub during the holidays.

FROTHY DRINKS

Bub is an Elizabethan slang word for a bubbling drink, and the essence of a syllabub is its frothy head. To achieve the effect, this method was suggested by the New Art of Cookery, published in 1792: "Put a bottle of either red or white wine . . . into a china bowl, sweeten it with sugar and grate in some nutmeg, then hold it under the cow, and milk into it till it has a fine froth at the top." There were whisks for those who didn't have a cow to make the froth, and 19th-century tinsmiths made syllabub churns for those who indulged often.

Syllabub continued to be a favorite drink

throughout the 1800s, particularly in New York, where the Dutch custom of paying New Year's Day visits still prevailed. Callers were always served refreshments; syllabub was often the beverage of choice.

Of these visits, novelist Lydia Maria Child wrote in 1842: "Every woman that is 'anybody' stays at home, dressed in her

best . . . and as every gentleman is honor bound to call on every lady whose acquaintance he does not intend to cut, the amount of eating and drinking done . . . must be very considerable. The number of calls is a matter of pride among ladies and there is considerable rivalry in the magnificence and variety of eating tables."

SYLLABUB

½ cup sugar
1 cup dry white wine, chilled
2 teaspoons finely shredded lemon peel
3 tablespoons lemon juice
1½ cups milk
1 cup light cream
Freshly grated nutmeg
2 egg whites
2 tablespoons sugar

■ Stir together ½ cup sugar, wine, lemon peel, and juice till sugar dissolves. In a large bowl combine milk, cream, and wine mixture. Beat with a rotary beater till smooth and frothy. Pour into bowl; top with freshly grated nutmeg. Beat egg whites with 2 tablespoons sugar till stiff peaks form. Spoon puffs of egg white on top of syllabub. Ladle into cups; serve with spoons. Makes 8 (½-cup) servings.

HOLIDAY FOLK ART

Handcraftsmanship never is more appropriate than during the holidays. Folk art removes winter's chill from the home and readies it for the season—and makes a great gift, too.

SANTAS

Rebecca Satter's handmade Belsnickles and Old World Santas aren't the ruddy-cheeked, jolly old souls most Americans have come to expect. They are expressions of Christmas from another culture.

Sometimes, the most unmomentous events are the catalysts that change a life. For Rebecca Satter, it was a phone call—and a *Country Home*® magazine cover. Life hasn't been the same since.

The phone call was from a friend wanting a favor. "She wanted a special Christmas present and wanted to know if I could make her an old-fashioned Santa. That was the beginning for me," recalls Rebecca.

Having never made a Santa before, Rebecca searched for resources. A trip to the library produced a December, 1985, *Country Home*, which had a brigade of unusual old-world and antique Santas marching across its cover.

Fascinated with these unusual emblems of Christmas, Rebecca wasn't content to craft only one. Handmade Belsnickles and Santas of intriguing character and meticulous detail are now her full-time business— and have been, ever since a friend took a few to a gift show in Los Angeles in 1986 and returned with 120 orders.

Immersing herself in research at her home in the gentle, mountainous countryside of southeastern Idaho, Rebecca discovered a world far removed from the American West—a world of European traditions and ethnic folklore she had not even suspected, prior to her nascent interest in old-world Christmas figures.

"[The *Country Home* article] was my first exposure to the Belsnickle," says Rebecca. "I always thought that the whole world celebrated a short, stocky, jovial kind of guy. But the German Belsnickle made me realize that the whole world did not celebrate Christmas the same way. I was very captivated."

Instead of the merry, rotund man with twinkling eyes and a kind heart, Rebecca found a European St. Nicholas who was solemn and somewhat unapproachable—traits realistic for the actual man, who had been a bishop in the fourth century.

Likewise, the Dutch *Sinterklaas* was no warmer a character. Although he, according to legend, rewarded good Dutch children with

Left: *Rebecca's Belsnickles are made from scraps of vintage clothing and are always trimmed in fur. The translation of "Belsnickle," in fact, is "St. Nicholas wearing fur."*

Right: *Horsehair forms the Belsnickle's beard and hair—a final detail to the clay-sculpted, carefully painted face.*

treats in their wooden shoes left waiting for his arrival on St. Nicholas Eve, he still was stone-faced and reserved—a father, more than a dad.

But it was the German culture and its tradition of the Belsnickle that truly enchanted Rebecca. "Doing research I became quite interested not only in the European folklore but also the folklore that came with the immigrants to America," she says. "German culture was strong on the East Coast during the 19th century, and that's the

era that historically interests me the most."

The Belsnickle takes his name from *Pelz-Nickolaus*, meaning "St. Nicholas in fur." But beyond this, history assigns no special dress to the figure. For Rebecca, this is an invitation to creativity.

She cuts each of her own Belsnickles and Santas from wood with a handsaw, then layers them with fiber filling. She molds clay for the hands and face with household items like toothpicks and cotton swabs. After drying the faces in the oven, Rebecca paints them with acrylics and applies layers of protective resin. Antique fur and fabric are used to clothe the figures—each one, proof that Christmas can be more than merry.

Opposite: *Wearing his familiar crimson coat and jovial spirits, Santa Claus is one of Rebecca's most popular figures. This one is designed to sit atop a mantel—ideally, above a crackling fire.*

Top: *Rebecca's Belsnickles are modeled after the formidable German figure who stalked through the snow, rewarding good children and punishing the bad.*

Above: *Rebecca makes miniature clothes for her Christmas figures on an old-fashioned treadle sewing machine from her home in southeastern Idaho.*

WOOD-CARVED SANTAS

When Californian Paul Bolinger takes a knife to wood, he crafts distinctive, stylized Santas that resonate with the spirit and feeling of their creator.

Beneath rosy cheeks, abject eyes, or stern mouths, Paul Bolinger's wood-carved Santas reverberate with a discomforting sense of life.

Make no mistake, Paul's Santas are not realistic. Each one is stylized—and a clear confirmation of Paul's wooden medium.

But still, the resonance of these figures suggests something more than wood, more than the tug of a knife across wood. Paul's wood sculptures seem to point, instead, to the spirit and feeling of the person holding the knife. To Paul himself.

It is this personal quality—literally, Paul's handprint—that distinguishes his Santas from the carvings of other craftspersons. It may even be this quality, or the opportunity for self-expression it represents, that compels Paul to bring Santas to life from wood, again and again.

"I honestly can't say why I spend so much time and effort on carving," he says. "But I get a terrific sense of satisfaction from finishing each one."

Carving offers at least one easily identifiable lure for Paul: simple escape, after a hard workday in the semiconductor industry.

It's an escape he has to make room for, however. "I share a playroom with my 6-year-old son, Jake," he explains.

Each figure takes from eight to 24 hours to carve from basswood. "It's repetitious," admits Paul, "but it's also a process of constant, small improvements."

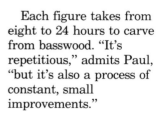

Opposite: *The array of Santas Paul has carved point to his dream: someday turning the hobby into a full-time career.*

Left: *Each Christmas figure takes Paul from eight to 24 hours to carve out of basswood.*

Below: *Paul Bolinger relaxes from a high-pressure, high-tech workday by spending three or four hours carving Santas at his Mountain View, California, home.*

FABRIC SANTA AND ANGEL ORNAMENTS

James Cramer couldn't find Christmas decorations appropriate for his rustic farmhouse, so he created his own. The result: primitive fabric Santas and angels that he now crafts full time.

Several adages come to mind when considering James Cramer's fabric Santas and angels—traditional ones, like "if you want the job done right, do it yourself." Or, a variation on an old idea: "You can take James Cramer's Christmas crafts out of the house, but you can't take the house out of James Cramer's Christmas crafts."

Whatever its formulation, the idea is the same: James' folk-art fabric Christmas figures and his home—a circa-1830s restored farmhouse in Keedysville, Maryland—are inseparable.

Just as soil nurtures seed, the rustic farmhouse was the fecund field in which James cultivated his talents as a folk artist. Until he bought the home in 1986, he had never

made a single one of the primitive Santas and angels he now creates from fabric as a full-time craft.

The character of the house—a no-frills structure meticulously restored to its stolid roots—demanded a

Above: *Among the carefully detailed Christmas figures that James has crafted is this angel in an Indian blanket, which adorns his attic studio.*

Left: *One of James' Santas is perfectly at home in an antique cupboard, alongside his collection of circa-1890 German carved sheep.*

FABRIC SANTA AND ANGEL ORNAMENTS

similarly no-nonsense approach when it was time to decorate for Christmas.

"I started this because I was tired of seeing so many Victorian Santas. They all look the same. For a house like mine, you need something else, a folksy look," James explains.

The fact is, when James first attempted to decorate his home for Christmas, he turned up empty-handed. The type of primitive decorations that would work in such a rugged, straightforward house simply weren't to be found. James didn't begin crafting holiday decorations just for the fun of it, then, so much as he did out of necessity.

Repulsed by froufrou holiday figurines and even the ubiquitous jolly fat Santas that grace most homes, James set out to create something different. Something that in no way would smack of a visual cliché.

His resulting repertoire of Santas defies our traditional images. Who'd envision Santa donning a southwestern Indian blanket in place of his de rigueur red velvet suit? Or Santa cloaked as a shepherd? These are just some of the punches James' freewheeling Santas audaciously pull.

In their features, too, his Santas, angels, and other Christmas figures defy popular preconceptions. For one thing, they seem almost unfinished—something of an Impressionistic suggestion of a face, instead of a realistic rendering.

The materials James uses also are rustic and natural, imbuing his creations with a different flavor than most figures in the genre. Twine, not a shiny black patent leather, binds a Santa's waistline. A barren grapevine wreath, not a lush evergreen one with a cheery Christmas bow, is carried by his Santa.

Its origins out of necessity may account for the success of James' craft: Apparently he wasn't the only one who believed there was a need for folksier figures to spread Christmas cheer around a historic home.

Above left: *James Cramer began crafting his own primitive Christmas angels and Santas from fabric when his search for holiday decorations for his rustic, historic home proved futile.*

Above: *The first Santa ever made by James has sentimental value: "I can't bear to sell it," he insists.*

Opposite: *James' Santas ignore the conventional red-velvet dress code, wearing southwestern blankets tied with twine. Their unique character further comes from James' use of natural materials and his refusal to "finish" features in the detailed, precise way that's expected.*

WOOD CARVINGS

From his circa-1820 rural home known as Christmas Tree Farm in Cutler, Maine, wood-carver Huston Clark Sieburth harvests Christmas sculptures from Maine's native pines using old-fashioned hand tools.

Despite its name, Christmas Tree Farm isn't the place to pay a fee and cut your own Christmas tree from grounds dense with balsam fir or sweet-smelling spruce, though plenty of both grow here. Instead, the Cutler, Maine, property hosts a different harvest of woods—the kind fashioned by a small knife, not felled by an ax.

As the home of wood-carver Huston Clark Sieburth, the circa-1820 house in the remote reaches of coastal Maine, halfway to the North Pole and mainly barren of people, provides a steady outpouring of folk wood sculpture year-round, not just at Christmas.

When Clark and his wife, Carole, first looked at their future home in 1984, its plethora of conifers and their own love of Christmas inspired the name. Christmas Tree Farm proved a serendipitous sobriquet when, one year later, Clark began a new vocation as a full-time wood-carver with a specialization in Father Christmases and Santas.

Previously he had been a professional magician, cook, and baker. But when Carole requested a Christmas carving as her present after moving to Cutler, it presaged a new career—one launched on a $20 nest egg.

Above: *Clark carves native pine with hand tools in his Cutler, Maine, home.*

Left: *Although Clark specializes in Santa Clauses and Father Christmases, his repertoire is not limited to these. Patriotic chickens, roosters, pumpkins, and fish fill in the seasonal gaps.*

Clark's entrée into the full-time vocation of wood carving by no means signaled his first effort at forming wood with a knife. He received his first whittling tools when he was only 5 years old, from his father, and he has carved ever since. He had never attempted anything as complicated as a human figure, though, until he carved the Father Christmas for Carole.

By the following spring, wood carving wasn't merely something to while away the long Maine winters. It was a full-fledged career.

"I am self-taught," says Clark of his new career, "both in carving and painting. I work in native white pine using only hand tools, and my work is known for my fine detail and original designs."

Maine is famous for its pine—in fact, it's known as the Pine Tree State—and Clark appropriately carves only this indigenous wood for his figures. Maine also is known for its time-honored tradition of wood carving, and Clark is happy to be a contemporary link in that venerable continuum.

"But I am not trying to re-create a legacy, as in reproduction work. I am attempting to create a new one," Clark insists.

Like the carvers of old,

Clark approaches his work armed only with hand tools—no quick-fix power equipment permitted.

"I use hand tools because I feel that the quality of the work I produce can be produced by no other methods. I still do all of the carving and painting myself [even though the business has grown] and will continue to do so," he says.

Clark and his family have an abiding interest in traditional Christmas celebrations from around the world and each year incorporate themes from other countries into their own observation of the holiday. The special significance international Christmas festivities have for Clark can be seen in his work.

"My Father Christmases and Santas are inspired by many different ethnic and regional traditions," he says. Carole confirms that the old-world flavor is well-received: "Many people of European descent identify figures of Clark's and are quite excited by them. His Father Christmases strike a responsive note with people who view them." At Christmas Tree Farm, the seasonal harvest continues year-round.

Above: *Who says Santa has to ride a reindeer—especially when a rooster's close at hand? Clark's wry humor imbues his carvings with an inimitable style.*

Above left: *The figurative emblems of Christmas can be rotund and massive or slim and elongated, like this Father Christmas.*

Opposite: *Often, Clark's Father Christmases stand on plinths shared with whimsical carved animals.*

MINIATURE LOG HOMES

Crafted a century ago to decorate beneath the Christmas tree, miniature log homes are being made anew by Dean Johnson—for gifts, as well as for decoration.

Pups, kittens, and kids are proof enough: There's an irresistible charm in the diminutive. The same principle holds for homes. If a full-size log home has rustic appeal, how much more so a pint-size version—one scaled down to easily fit atop a table within yet another log home, like Chinese nesting boxes?

Dean Johnson felt the allure of miniature dwellings 10 years ago, when he started collecting tiny antique homes made from general-store crates. His admiration prompted him to action. Five years ago, Dean began making the miniatures himself. Now, his hold-in-your-hand architecture is a collectible of its own.

His first piece was a birdhouse he built from scrap wood, but he has also constructed a Noah's ark, farmhouses, and even a rugged miniature mill with a working waterwheel.

"The most elaborate thing I've tried so far was building a church," says

Dean. "The doors opened up and you could see the choir inside."

At Christmas, Dean's downsize dwellings have special significance. Miniature log cabins from the late 1800s originally were crafted by fathers for their sons to put under the Christmas trees for decoration.

In the spirit of those early crafters, Dean builds his own miniatures from cast-off materials—many of which come from the restoration of his home in rural Maryland.

Creating his folk art demands real commitment. Dean has a full-time job, and his woodwork must be fit in during leisure. "I'm putting in about 70 hours a week now on both my regular job and making my small log cabins," Dean says.

Until he moved his equipment from a shed to a heated garage, the craft had its chilly moments. "If your fingers are cold, hammering and nailing isn't much fun."

Above: *This Noah's ark, a commissioned piece, is one of Dean's more elaborate works.*

Right: *Dean Johnson builds his miniature dwellings in his free time—a situation he hopes to soon change.*

Opposite: *Dean's first effort at miniature dwellings was a birdhouse crafted from pieces of lath salvaged from the restoration of his Maryland farmhouse.*

PAINTINGS

*Scenes from the winter wonderland of her youth—rural Michigan—
permeate folk painter Kathy Jakobsen's vibrant portrait of simple
American country life.*

Even when a career breakthrough meant eight years of speed-lane living in New York City, Americana painter Kathy Jakobsen never lost her slow-motion vision—one of fat, fluffy snowflakes lazily floating down and ensconcing themselves like visiting royalty on the whitecapped countryside of rural Michigan.

Or her mental picture of plaid-shirted men bundled in winter hats and boots and huddled in open-faced wooden huts where they fished through holes carved in the ice.

These are just some of the scenes from her bucolic past that spill through Kathy's mind and onto her canvasses.

Kathy was born in 1952 in Wyandotte, Michigan, a suburb of Detroit that was then wide-open and capacious—roomy enough for Kathy, as a child, to explore a cache of simple, rural pleasures that would leave an indelible imprint on her sensibilities and, ultimately, on her art.

"We had over an acre of land, and my neighbors had a horse that I

practically called my own. I really loved that horse," says Kathy. "Now I always put horses in my paintings. Even when I paint city scenes, I'll include a mounted policeman or a carriage."

On each of her country-life canvases, the colors

are at once dreamlike, soothing as a child's lullabye with their harmonious blends and balance, yet vibrant, luminous as an enchanted forest.

In one of Kathy's winter scenes, for example, billows of snow

Above: *Kathy Jakobsen paints her scenes of Americana in oils from a simple oak table in her Michigan home.*

Opposite: *A treasure-trove of childhood memories, this Christmas painting captures the essence of Kathy's early days in Michigan.*

PAINTINGS

form an undulating rhythm across the canvas with their interplay of blue-tinged white and deeper blue-black shadows—colors lambent and magical. A thin peel of peach at the horizon cracks the seemingly impenetrable winter-blue sky, bridging it and the snowy hills with a pastel promise of sunlight.

Often, details are Kathy's favorite themes from childhood—a snowman with twig arms and a red striped scarf; a young boy stretched out in the snow, alongside the "snow angel" imprint he's just made in the deep powder; dogs and cats prancing along snowy fields and lanes; ice skaters cutting a striking silhouette on a frozen pond; a family, snug beneath a blanket, enjoying a sleigh ride behind a horse wearing a red harness of sleigh bells.

Details imbue Kathy's work with a distinctive resonance. This same representational approach, however, nearly frustrated her to a screeching halt as an artist in college.

"I was developing my own style, which might be called naive but to me was just the simple colorful things I liked to paint. Anyway, it was a time when abstract and fine art were really in, and my representational style was considered worthless," she says.

"Although I grew up with art, my attempt at formal training was a complete disaster. I remember our final project in one class. The instructor was supposed to walk down the aisles and comment about

everyone's artwork, but when he got to mine he just glanced down and then walked on without saying anything. It was the ultimate put-down."

Enough of one that Kathy began searching for "real" work. She thought about enrolling in a business machine course, but then realized "what a terrible thing it was to postulate your own failure. And I thought, *I'm not going to fail.* I chose to make it go right with art no matter what," she says.

Kathy turned to calligraphy, then to fraktur—Pennsylvania German illustration. She

was encouraged to paint by the late Dr. Robert Bishop, who went on to head the Museum of American Folk Art, which now has Kathy's work in its collection. When a Michigan friend opened a folk art gallery in Manhattan, he took Kathy's work with him. It was such a success that Kathy herself moved to the city.

These days she's back in Michigan, painting at the home she shares with her husband and child. She's come full circle, in life and in art. "Over the years, I've found that art, like life, is an ever-expanding experience. And I love it!"

Opposite: *Painted in 1984, "Shopping in Town" shows Kathy's appreciation for quaint, rural villages. Her childhood love of horses also gains expression with ample horse-drawn sleighs.*

Below: *Kathy's first oil paintings were scenes of winter ice fishing on Michigan's frozen lakes. The stylized trees and lake moss contribute to the painting's rhythm and balance, while details—a plaid flannel shirt—give the scene whimsy.*

TOYS

If anything spreads the magic of Christmas, it's old-fashioned toys. Randal Smith and Rebecca Shrode continue a time-honored tradition, making toys the early way from metal, wood, and fabric.

Above: *Randy carves toys from wood, which Rebecca then paints.*

Left: *Randal Smith and Rebecca Shrode have produced more than 100 different toy designs made of tin, wood, cast pewter, and fabric. The circa-1850 hand-powered rotary machine shown here bends tin, but most of their equipment is simple hand tools.*

Right: *An antique cabinet filled with Randy and Rebecca's wares attests to the joy of childhood, as well as to the range of this toy-making team.*

Toys are to Christmas as eggs are to Easter: synonymous with popular, if not religious, celebration. As high-tech leaves its impersonal trademark on American households, now more than ever, getting in touch with the childlike joy of Christmas demands looking to the past—often, to the toy trains and tin soldiers of erstwhile times—as a means of infusing the home with holiday magic.

A scattering of old-fashioned toys beneath the tree or atop a table is a sure way to invoke Christmas cheer, but a paucity—and, sometimes, the hefty price tags—of antique toys don't always make ownership of the authentic articles possible.

But not to despair. If Ohio toy-makers Rebecca Shrode and Randal Smith have anything to do with it, there'll be plenty of antique-style playthings to put heart into the holidays. Both are committed to making new toys in the old modes— and to spreading Christmas cheer in the process.

TOYS

He's a self-taught tinsmith: "I've always admired old toys. As a kid my grandparents got me started collecting tin soldiers. That fired my interest in metalworking. I nearly burned down my parents' kitchen a couple of times, playing around with casting techniques," Randy remembers.

In 1973, his childhood interest in tin finally paid off. He was hired as a tinsmith by Greenfield Village, the living-history museum at Dearborn, Michigan. While there, he taught himself even more about the craft, using the museum's collection of 19th-century hand tools.

Randy left Greenfield Village to make his way as an itinerant craftsman. At a crafts show in 1983, he met Rebecca, and the two became business partners.

Together, they create not only tin toys, which Randy designs, but also toys made from wood and fabric, based on Rebecca's designs. Most of their offerings are either accurate reproductions or adaptations of early toys. Some of the metal playthings are even cast in antique molds.

"As the price of antique toys went up and up, I decided that there should be a market among the starting collectors for quality museum reproductions," explains Randy. So far, the market likes what this toy-making team produces—especially the childlike magic it brings to Christmas.

Above: *Pewter and tin pull-toys are cast reproductions of mass-produced toys. The antique Tom Thumb riding a dog was manufactured in the 1860s.*

Right: *Wooden toy soliders carved by Randy and painted by Rebecca are authentically clothed according to war and regiment.*

CHRISTMAS TRAVELER

Celebrate the season at one of America's historic villages, where long-lost traditions live on. Preserved for all to enjoy, the beloved memories of Christmases past ring loud and clear.

COLONIAL WILLIAMSBURG

Capture the Christmas spirit as it prevailed in the 1700s. Holiday festivities were not all that filled the minds of Colonial Americans, as this historic village attests.

Freshly fallen snow dusts the cobblestone streets of Colonial Williamsburg, Virginia, framing the 18th-century houses with a blanket of shimmering white. Bands of carolers march with joyous rhythm through the bustling town. Nearly every house wears a festive coat of holiday color—wreaths and garlands festooned with fresh fruit.

By dusk, the mood reaches fever pitch. Children race to follow the gay strains of fife and drum. Suddenly, a cannon booms and within an instant the entire town is filled with the light of hundreds of candles and the fiery glow of cressets. Christmas at Colonial Williamsburg has begun.

The Grand Illumination, held each year in early December, heralds the start of the holiday season at Colonial Williamsburg with 18th-century-style fireworks, music, and entertainment. Such feasting and revelry is a popular tradition

in a village held fast by the traditions of an earlier era.

Colonial Williamsburg re-creates the town of Williamsburg as it appeared on the eve of the American Revolution. From 1699 to 1780, Williamsburg was the capital of Virginia— England's oldest, largest, richest, and most populous colony. The settlement cradled, in a sense, the seeds of a fledgling nation and served as a training ground for Virginians primed for independence.

Some 2,000 people lived in Williamsburg during its colonial heyday. Although small by modern standards, the capital city was considered at the time to be the epicenter of political power, fashion, trade, and intellectualism.

Within the town's shops, taverns, homes, and streets, Virginia patriots such as Thomas Jefferson, Patrick Henry, and George Mason lived and worked. Their

Above: *Swaddled in greens and topped with a wreath, this cheery blue door receives a typical holiday dressing. As a part of its yuletide program, Colonial Williamsburg offers tours that highlight the town's special holiday decorations.*

Right: *The Governor's Palace is the site of outdoor stage performances at Christmastime. Begun by Lt. Gov. Edward Nott in 1706 and completed in 1722, it is one of 50 major structures rebuilt on their original sites, plus 88 original buildings that have been restored.*

COLONIAL WILLIAMSBURG

colonial life-style—restored and reconstructed today in more than 400 public and private buildings—provides visitors with a captivating glimpse at a nation on the brink of monumental change.

Williamsburg's role as a cultural powerhouse diminished once Jefferson transferred Virginia's government to Richmond during the revolution. Without political fervor to fuel its existence, Williamsburg settled into a peaceful, perhaps unremarkable, community.

But in 1926, the Reverend Dr. W. A. R. Goodwin brought Williamsburg to the forefront once again. As rector of Bruton Parish Church, Goodwin saw potential in Williamsburg's time-worn frame houses and ramshackle tenements, and imagined the revitalized slice of history that might one day stand in their place.

Goodwin shared his vision with John D. Rockefeller, Jr., who eventually supported and financed Williamsburg's restoration. The museums and grounds held a special place in Rockefeller's heart until his death in 1960.

Today, the Colonial Williamsburg Foundation oversees the largest museum program in the world. More than one million visitors tour the site each year. The Historic Area encompasses 173 of Williamsburg's original 220 acres. Researchers modeled the site after a 1781 map used to billet French troops during the Yorktown siege.

Above: *Visitors are invited to join the bands of costumed carolers who roam the streets of Colonial Williamsburg during the holiday season. Other groups often gather at the Courthouse to sing by the light of bonfires and cressets.*

Right: *The season being cold and frosty, a hearty meal is a welcome diversion. Special Christmas buffets, breakfasts, and dinners are served at the four taverns in the Historic Area. Meals feature traditional colonial fare—all served on reproduction table settings. This centerpiece is a colonial classic.*

The combined talents of archaeologists, architects, and historical researchers were used to re-create an accurate picture of the colonial era. Data were collected from deeds, wills, insurance contracts, letters, diaries, and photographs. Existing 18th-century houses were analyzed in detail—from the latches on their doors to the mortar in their chimneys.

More than 50 buildings and structures—such as the Capitol and the Governor's Palace—have been reconstructed on their original sites. These are in addition to the 88 original buildings.

Although this town-size museum is open year-round, there's no season to visit quite like Christmas. Visitors are treated to candlelight concerts nearly every day. Carolers spread Christmas joy from the steps of the Courthouse at twilight. Special holiday exhibits, tours, and programs take place throughout the town.

Many folks travel to Colonial Williamsburg simply to admire the trappings of Christmas. You can tour the festively decorated town, bedecked at nearly every turn with fruits and greens. You can even attend a holiday decorating workshop in addition to some 40 regular exhibits and activities.

At Christmastime, as throughout the year, visitors can tour 225 rooms furnished with antique and reproduction furniture and accessories from the museum's 100,000-piece collection. You'll find rooms outfitted with 1700s bedsteads wrapped in William and Mary coverlets. Reproduction fabrics —silk velvet, damask, and linen—cover the chairs and beds, and are used for draperies and clothing. Every detail, from candlesnuffers to cornices, is historically accurate.

Costumed interpreters bake bread, build furniture, spin wool, weave cloth, print books, and make implements at 17 trade sites and compounds.

In addition to the Historic Area, the museum also includes the DeWitt Wallace Decorative Arts Gallery, which features 8,000 objects from the 17th to 19th centuries, the Abby Aldrich Rockefeller Folk Art Center, Bassett Hall (home of the Rockefeller family), and Carter's Grove, an 800-acre plantation documenting four centuries of Virginia history.

For those who long for the warmth and merriment of Christmases past, a visit to Colonial Williamsburg will be a trip to treasure.

Holiday festivities run from early December through New Year's. For more information, write or call: Christmas Events, Visitor Center, Colonial Williamsburg, P.O. Box 1776, Williamsburg, VA 23187-1776; 804/220-7368 or 804/220-7738.

CONNER PRAIRIE

Take a candlelight tour of Christmas Eve celebrations at Prairietown, Indiana, and discover how the holidays in this simple little town differ from the full-blown pageantry we know and love today.

Harriet Campbell arranges a few sprigs of red cedar in the dining room of her home in Prairietown, Indiana, in a humble attempt to add some Christmas color and cheer. She recalls the grand balls and Christmas parties enjoyed in Lexington, Kentucky, in seasons past. Harriet remembers, too, the years spent in her home state of Virginia, where the Episcopal Church she attended as a child was always gaily decorated for Christmas Day services. Harriet longs now for the huge banquets of holiday food and the never-ending stream of visitors she so vividly remembers. But here in Prairietown—the fictional village created at Conner Praire living history museum—Harriet has no wreaths of green nor children to indulge this Christmas. The year is 1836 and in this Midwestern village located four hours by horse from downtown Indianapolis (30 minutes by car today) the now-

familiar notions of Christmas are only beginning to take root.

The Christmas holiday was not uniformly celebrated in America during the mid-1800s. The extent of the celebration depended largely on people's religious beliefs, their backgrounds, and the area of the country in which they lived. In Midwestern villages such as Prairietown, Christmas was neither a community extravaganza or a great celebration of the church.

Nevertheless, Harriet Campbell lays some

Above: The Curtis family brought to Prairietown a host of Christmas traditions from their native New York State. They hang stockings by the fire, enjoy a visit from Santa on Christmas Eve, and share a huge family meal on Christmas Day.

Left: Nineteenth-century prices are preserved at Prairietown. A mere 12½ cents reserves sleeping space in the common chamber at the Golden Eagle Tavern—one of some 30 historical buildings transported to Conner Prairie's 1836 village.

CONNER PRAIRIE

special foods upon her table for friends and neighbors who were invited to stop by. She and her husband, Dr. Campbell, the town physician, hope to lead a few rousing choruses of old English carols such as *The First Noel* and *God Rest Ye Merry Gentlemen.*

Harriet and Dr. Campbell are just two of the 100 people who re-create 19th-century life at Conner Prairie. An entire village of characters—each created from a composite of historical information—play the roles of carpenter, blacksmith, schoolmaster, widow, innkeeper, and the like. They live in authentic homes, wear period clothing, and use historical tools, furniture, and household items. Villagers often strike up conversations with the visitors passing through, mimicking the attitudes and mannerisms of the year 1836.

Interpreters at the village also re-create everyday happenings such as weddings, funerals, patriotic celebrations, and other seasonal events.

During its annual candlelight tour, Conner Prairie invites visitors to witness firsthand how the diverging views of Christmas play out in this Midwestern community. The Ben Curtis family, for example, enjoys one of the most exuberant Christmas celebrations in town, following traditions brought with them from their home in New York State. Stockings hang by the chimney and special gifts await each of the three children. Even Santa himself will make a surprise visit on

Christmas Eve. Ben closes his blacksmithing shop on Christmas Day and invites his apprentice and helper to join in the family meal.

In contrast, Alex and Grace Fenton snarl at the thought of drinking, fireworks, or any type of Christmas celebration. Because their religious upbringing warns against such frivolous festivities, the couple chooses instead to spend the day as they would any other. Their neighbors won't mind, however. Folks in town are used to the couple's somewhat unusual ways.

If the Fentons are sick, for example, they insist on healing themselves with herbal medicines rather than following the advice of Dr. Campbell.

The townspeople are only a part of the historical atmosphere at Conner Prairie, which was founded in 1964 when pharmaceutical heir Eli Lilly donated the William Conner home and surrounding land to Earlham College in Richmond. The 1836 village now comprises more than 30 historical buildings, moved to the site in the 1970s.

Conner's home is still the centerpiece of Conner Prairie. The son of a fur trader whose first wife, Mekinges, was a Delaware Indian, Conner lived and worked alongside the tribes for most of his life. By the time he'd built his Federal-style home in 1823, however, Conner had made the transition from a life among the Indians to that of an entrepreneur/politician in the white man's world.

Within his tidy brick estate, Conner and his

second wife, Elizabeth Chapman, raised a large family as well as entertaining legislators and other important politicians.

Their home looks today much as it did more than 150 years ago. A huge hearth, covered with authentic utensils, warms the kitchen. The dining room, parlor, and upstairs bedrooms are filled with reproduction furniture and antiques. A visit to the Loom House out back reveals the 19th-century techniques used to weave blankets and coverlets. And inside Conner Barn resides a herd of lambs that are much like the ones that might have grazed on the property in decades past.

Above: *An authentic 1830s meal awaits visitors at the William Conner home. Guests are invited to help bake the biscuits, grind coffee, and churn butter.*

The Pioneer Adventure Area at Conner Prairie allows visitors the chance to spin, weave, make soap, comb wool, and try many of the activities that occupied daily pioneer life. Children particularly love sitting in the old wooden desks at the District Schoolhouse and imagining a typical day in this 1800s classroom.

Interpreters at the Pioneer Barn demonstrate how strenuous farming in the 1800s could be. Visitors are encouraged to lend a hand with many of

the chores. On theme weekends, activities highlight some of the more playful aspects of pioneer life: puppet shows, spelling bees, and corn husk doll and punched tin craft workshops.

At Christmastime, the aromas of a hearthside supper permeate the William Conner house. Guests are invited to help prepare a feast of typical 1830s fare, such as corn chowder, chicken and dumplings, brown bread and apple butter, and spicy gingerbread. The evening's entertainment includes playing classic 19th-century parlor games and joining in the enlightening banter of costumed interpreters.

Ask your hosts about current events and

they're quick to recount tales of the battle at the Alamo or to offer an opinion on their new president, Martin Van Buren. Inquire, however, about the influence of the Civil War or telephones and you'll likely be met with innocently blank stares. For the characters at Prairietown who bring the year 1836 to life, putting food on the table, keeping the family healthy, and finishing the evening's chores are worry enough.

Christmas tours are conducted from early December through the 23rd. For more information, write or call: Conner Prairie, 13400 Allisonville Rd., Noblesville, IN 46060; 317/776-6000.

Top: *The glow of candlelight illuminates the schoolhouse on a winter's night. This one-room school—moved here in 1970— was originally used in Kosciousko County, Indiana.*

Above: *Nighttime tours allow visitors to see the events of a typical 1830s Christmas Eve, such as this woman reading her Bible by firelight.*

OLD SALEM

Home to the largest Moravian congregation in the Western Hemisphere, the historic district of Old Salem, North Carolina, cradles Christmas traditions celebrated long ago in a faraway land.

Since its birth as a religious center for the Moravian Church in 1766, Salem, North Carolina, has offered peace to all who gather here. In the mid-1700s, a handful of pioneers chose the unsettled lands of North Carolina in which to plant the foundations of a Protestant church conceived 500 years earlier in Europe. They built towns such as Bethania and Bethabara before taking root in Salem, the carefully planned village that became the center of Moravian religious, cultural, and social life.

Today in Old Salem—the historic district that preserves the original town—church, work, and family are still revered. Christmas here may be simple in scale, but the emotions behind it run 200 years deep.

An Old Salem Christmas (set between 1790 and 1830) is heralded with the traditional Candle Tea, held the first two Thursdays, Fridays, and Saturdays after Thanksgiving. Central to the Candle Tea is the making of the *putz* (a

German word meaning *"to decorate"*)—typically a model of the nativity. This early Moravian custom is practiced today in one of Old Salem's nine major buildings open to the public. Visitors are greeted by the sounds of Christmas carols played on a 1797 organ, and the scents of beeswax and fresh-baked sugar cake and ginger cookies. Through flickering candlelight, guests see not only a traditional nativity, much like those fashioned by early Moravian families, but a model of the village of Salem as well.

The miniature houses in this model—stacked in tidy rows along narrow streets—illustrate the care with which Salem was settled. The town's founders arrived in Salem by a circuitous route that led from their homeland in Moravia (now part of Czechoslovakia) to religious freedom in Germany, and finally to the colonies of the New World.

The group's first attempt at settling in Georgia in 1735 failed. A second try in Bethlehem, Pennsylvania, seven years

later brought the Moravians recognition as solid citizens whose talents as master craftspeople were highly sought. Their reputation prompted an invitation from one of the governing officials of Carolina colony, encouraging the group to settle permanently in his territory.

To the tract of North Carolina, which they dubbed Wachovia, the Moravians brought a strong work ethic, a love of music, a belief in education for both men and women, and a dream of a utopian life that would allow them to work and worship in peace.

Unfettered by religious and social constraints, the people of Salem practiced a Christmas tradition rich with old-world heritage and warmth. Today, Old Salem Christmas—a

Above: *The structures at Old Salem in Winston-Salem, North Carolina, reflect the European roots of their builders. Typical homes had tile roofs, central chimneys, and asymmetrical windows.*

Opposite: *The Moravian settlers who established Old Salem were renowned for their love of music. Musical performances are enjoyed by visitors throughout the year.*

series of holiday events revives the Christmas customs of years past. As always, visitors to Old Salem can see some two dozen cooking, crafts, and trade demonstrations, and learn about the daily life of the colonial families and individuals who sought refuge here. During this special celebration, the historic village wears its ethnic colors like no other time of year.

Simple decorations and swags of greenery decorate the homes and shops. Sixty-five historical buildings have been restored or reconstructed at Old Salem, some of which are prepared especially for public tours. These include the Single Brothers House (built for single men and boys), Miksch Tobacco Shop, Winkler Bakery, Boys School, a firehouse, the restored

home of a clockmaker and silversmith, Salem Tavern and Barn, Shultz Shoemaker Shop, and Dr. Benjamin Vierling Apothecary and Home.

Wooden pyramids laden with greens, fruit, decorated Bible verses, and candles are a classic Old Salem decoration that captures the simple ceremony of early Moravian Christmases. Paintings or drawings known as illuminations are another favorite. These delicate depictions of the nativity come to life when lit from behind by candlelight.

Old Salem draws people of all faiths to its churches at Christmastime to join in the beloved tradition of lovefeasts. These gatherings are patterned after the 18th-century *agape*, the practice

whereby believers join together to break bread as a symbol of their unity and equality. Modern-day lovefeasts rely less on ceremony (they usually involve sharing simple refreshments), but the spirit of community and fellowship these events evoke is as strong as ever.

The Christmas festivities at Old Salem culminate with the lovefeasts and church services that take place on Christmas Eve. As people arrive, the churches are dark. Everyone receives unlit candles, which are lighted, one by one, until the church radiates with a flickering glow. To the people who gather here each Christmas, and to those who have gathered in Christmases past, these flames of love spreading joy and light to all the

world epitomize the Old Salem experience.

Holiday events at Old Salem begin a week after Thanksgiving and run through the third week in December. For information, contact: Old Salem Inc., Box F, Winston-Salem, NC 27108; 919/721-7300.

Above: Cooking demonstrations reveal the secrets of such Moravian Christmas classics as sugar cake and ginger cookies. Although life on the frontier was arduous, people still found time to savor these delightful treats.

Right: Moravian craftspeople had a reputation for quality work. Many of their homes, originally built in the 1700s, endured well into the 20th century, when efforts were first made to preserve and restore this historic settlement.

GREENFIELD VILLAGE

It's December, time for the voices of Christmas past to spread the yuletide spirit throughout the visionary village created by automobile magnate Henry Ford.

The warmth of a Christmas fire burning brightly softened the chilly winds that cut across the barren fields and isolated homesteads of Columbiana County, Ohio, during the early years on the American frontier.

In the 1820s brick farmhouse where he was born, Harvey Firestone, founder of the Firestone Tire and Rubber Company, weathered winter's icy grip and forged a character that would one day mark him as a leader and entrepreneur.

At Greenfield Village— the 81-acre living history museum in Dearborn, Michigan, where Firestone's birthplace now stands—Christmas envelopes the home with the happy ring of children's voices, the lingering scents of homemade foods, and the jingle of horse and sleigh. The holiday season is joyous and bright at Greenfield

Above: *Not every dwelling at Greenfield Village is trimmed this elegantly at Christmastime. The decorations in some of the earlier-era homes are appropriately spartan.*

Left: *The Firestone Farm depicts agricultural life in this country in the late 19th century. This 1828 farmhouse is the birthplace of Harvey Firestone, founder of the Firestone Tire and Rubber Company.*

GREENFIELD VILLAGE

Village. Yet, the harsh realities of pioneer life also are preserved as a gentle reminder of the milestones in American development.

Harvey Firestone is not the only American hero honored at Greenfield Village. Henry Ford, inventor of the Model T car, founded Henry Ford Museum & Greenfield Village in 1929 as a way to showcase individuals and events that have advanced American life.

"I'm going to start up a museum and give people a true picture of the development of the country," Ford said. Here he brought together the fragmented mementos of an industrializing nation: the legendary laboratories of Thomas Edison, the boyhood home of Orville and Wilbur Wright, and the Connecticut house where Noah Webster completed his *American Dictionary of the English Language.*

Alone, these structures capture only a brief moment in history. But together, alongside some 80 other historic homes, shops, and buildings dating from the 17th to the 20th century, they tell a powerful story of tradition and time-honored values.

When lacy flakes of snow powder Greenfield Village, horse-drawn sleighs replace the wheeled vehicles on tours throughout the village. Each fresh layer of white wraps this historic settlement in a snug cocoon, buffering it further still from the complexities of modern-day living.

Inside the historical homes and businesses, the spirit of Christmas awaits.

Some homes are bedecked with all the extravagance their owners can muster. Others give only the slightest nod to the holiday season. Yet each is authentic for the period it depicts.

The Sunday parlor is dressed for the holidays at Henry Ford's birthplace. Dozens of candles, fruit, toys, and strings of popcorn drape the branches of the Christmas tree. Fresh garlands line the mantel above a fireplace. In the kitchen, costumed interpreters grind meat for homemade sausage.

They're cooking, too, at the Edison Homestead, as interpreters pull piping hot gingerbread from the wood-burning oven and homemade candy boils on the stove. Visitors are invited to take a copy of these heirloom recipes to try at home by more conventional methods.

History is plain to see at Greenfield Village, but that's not all. There is plenty of opportunity to touch, smell, and live the life-style of our ancestors—from making old-fashioned Christmas decorations to shucking corn on the farm. Ford's historical complex, known collectively as the Edison Institute, holds a wealth of American artifacts and inventions. The indoor Henry Ford Museum spans 12 acres and includes a world-renowned automobile

Right: *These tarts are prepared using historical utensils and baked in a wood-burning oven. At Christmastime, the delectable aromas of fresh-baked cookies and holiday candies fill the air.*

collection, planes, trains, machinery, and myriad pieces of Americana. Walk the tidy streets of the adjoining Greenfield Village and you'll find block after block of historic treasures.

The Historic homes area at the village traces the development of housing from a rustic log cabin to an urban boarding house. The 1620s Cotswold Cottage is the oldest home in the village. Stepping inside this sturdy stone home—with its two-foot-thick walls and limestone shingles— conjures up images of the rolling Cotswold Hills of England, where the house once stood, and of the sheepherder and his family who are thought to have lived there.

In contrast, visitors to the Edison Homestead discover labor-saving devices of the 19th century. Meals are prepared on a wood-burning stove rather than at the open hearth.

Thomas Edison's laboratory—moved board by board from Menlo Park, New Jersey—is a favorite stop. More than 400 inventions, including the incandescent light, were created here. Down the street, the Sarah Jordan Boarding House provides a glimpse at the home life of the Edison assistants, who lived in one of the first residences in the world to be wired for electric light.

Visitors can see history in action at the Trades and Manufactures area. Demonstrations of glass blowing, blacksmithing, printing, domestic crafts, and other trades take place on a regular basis.

Community buildings representing America's political, social, and religious life circle the Village Green. The Eagle Tavern was originally an 1850s stagecoach stop. It's still a popular watering hole, where authentic meals are dished up along with 19th-century hospitality.

Many of the village rides and exhibits are operated on a seasonal basis. In warmer months, Town Hall is head-quarters for frolicking fun on The Green. Dressed for the 1880s, interpreters or staff lead kids in chasing hoops and other old-time games. June through Labor Day, youngsters (and the young-at-heart) can take a twirl on the 1913 carousel at Suwanee Park, hop aboard a steamboat, and enjoy a sundae at the 1870 ice cream parlor. A final spin around the perimeter of Greenfield Village on a steam-powered locomotive is a fitting end to an exciting day.

Although summer is glorious at Greenfield Village, Christmastime is the season when the museum pulls out all the stops. The celebration is indeed memorable. Behind the historic storefronts and within the carefully restored homes survive the Christmas traditions of the past 350 years.

Christmas activities run from early December through the end of the month. For more information, contact: Henry Ford Museum & Greenfield Village, P.O. Box 1970, Dearborn, MI 48121-1970; 1-800-343-1929.

Above: *Christmas trees on display at Greenfield Village show how tree-trimming styles have changed through the years. This patriotic version is covered in American flags.*

Left: *From lightposts to living rooms, Greenfield Village gets gussied up for the holidays. Plan to spend a day touring the historic establishments in the village and sampling the activities there. You'll need another day to see the rest of the exhibits at the adjoining Henry Ford Museum.*

WINTERTHUR

Welcome to the family estate of Henry Francis du Pont, whose impeccable taste and exemplary collections of decorative arts guide the Christmas celebrations at his museum and home.

Christmas at Winterthur, the lavish Delaware estate of Henry Francis du Pont, is no simple celebration. Planned nearly a year in advance, the holiday season at this premier museum of the decorative arts is as comprehensive as the collections housed within its walls. There are so many decorated rooms—each historically accurate—that tour guides are a necessity to keep visitors from getting lost among the treasures.

The estate was built in 1839 by James Antoine and Evelina Gabrielle du Pont Bidermann. Although by no means humble, that home bears little resemblance to the modern-day version—a labyrinth of rooms brimming with an outstanding assortment of antiques and collectibles. The man responsible for the tranformation at Winterthur is Henry Francis du Pont, who inherited the estate in 1927 and, at the age of 46, decided to convert it into a museum for his ever-growing collections. As his acquisitions grew, so did his home.

What began as a 12-room house today spans nine floors and offers more than 55,000 square feet of space for displays. In some cases, du Pont salvaged entire rooms from historical houses awaiting the wrecking ball and installed them in his home. Against these backdrops he created rooms that express the social and cultural traditions of the era.

The Chinese Parlor, for example, is a fitting location for a Twelfth Night Party. The room's unusual hand-painted wallpaper matches the drama of this traditional holiday gala. The setting—like many of the those created especially for a Winterthur Christmas—includes reproduction foods (to last through the entire season). The earliest Twelfth Night cake was

Opposite: The elaborate gardens at Winterthur Museum sleep beneath a coat of white at Christmastime. This 1,000-acre estate, located in Wilmington, Delaware, is renowned for its spectacular gardens and interiors.

Above: A display of yuletide spirit welcomes visitors to Montmorenci Stair Hall and introduces them to the history of Christmas greens.

Right: The researchers at Winterthur found no precedent for hanging Christmas wreaths until the 1800s. Even in those days, however, elaborate celebrations like the ones seen at the museum were probably far more expensive than most Americans could afford.

WINTERTHUR

Right: *Bounty from the gardens surrounding Winterthur— including statis, lilies, zinnias, and marigolds—decorate the dried flower tree that is on display in the Conservatory.*

traditionally baked with a bean and a pea hidden within. The man who found the bean became the King of the Feast and the woman who discovered the pea was the Queen. Later, pictorial Twelfth Night cards, drawn from a hat, determined the King and Queen. The King could order the rest of the party to perform whatever shenanigans he chose—play charades, sing, dance, or whatever. The Queen typically made the cake the next year.

Decking the halls at Winterthur is an elaborate process, with two centuries of Christmases past accurately reproduced. To create each holiday setting, the staff draws upon the museum's vast collections of items used in the original 13 colonies from 1640 to 1860. A scene depicting a holiday dinner at the Mt. Vernon home of George Washington, for example, includes authentic porcelain pieces from the period. Other holiday vignettes might include artifacts ranging from needlework and hooked rugs to period furniture and pottery.

Although many of our popular Christmas traditions developed only in the last 150 years, early Americans were quite taken with the practice of feasting and gift-giving. Visitors to the museum literally step into these festive scenes as they

appeared centuries ago. You can glimpse an 1803 Christmas Eve wedding, attend elegant parties, even experience the ceremonial shooting in of the New Year. The ceremony originated long ago, when young men welcomed in the New Year by going from farm to farm, where one of them would chant a poem and the group would fire their guns to ward off evil spirits and issue in good luck and prosperity for the coming year. Families would then

invite the men inside for food and drink.

The holidays at Winterthur showcase an amalgam of traditions from our past: baking cookies, feasting on elaborate dinners, wrapping gifts in fancy papers, and decorating the Christmas tree. It seems unimaginable that only a century ago Christmas trees were rarely found in American homes. Yet within a few decades, the Christmas tree became not only a yuletide staple but also an

artistic and emotional expression of the season. By the 1930s, decorated evergreens in all shapes and sizes graced nearly every home.

Examples of early Christmas trees are a favorite attraction at the museum during the holidays. The Pennsylvania German Christmas tree is laden with matzebaum, a rectangular-shaped almond paste treat, and gingerbread cookies molded into animal forms. The first documented tree seen in America—a

Moravian tree made of a wooden pyramid covered with greens—stands in the Hall of Statues. The dried flower tree on display in the Conservatory is a tribute to Henry du Pont's love for his gardens.

Whether the mood is lavish or sedate, every room of the house celebrates—with colorful elegance and period authenticity—the pleasures of the season.

Yuletide tours are given from mid-November through early January. For more information, contact: Winterthur Information and Ticket Office, Winterthur, DE 19735; 800/448-3883.

Above: *The Twelfth Night feast awaits party guests in the Chinese Parlor. Recipes for holiday foods shown at Winterthur are available in the cookbook* Yuletide at Winterthur: Tastes and Visions of the Season.

Left: *Animal ornaments decorate the traditional Pennsylvania German tree and add to the warm and simple flavor of the Fraktur Room. Children typically gobbled these tasty ornaments as the tree was being dismantled.*

MYSTIC SEAPORT

Tall ships and tall tales drop anchor at Connecticut's seaport museum, which charms visitors with its lifelike portrayals of Christmas by the sea.

Christmas Day in 1929 was an optimistic day indeed for the residents of the seaside town of Mystic, Connecticut. While the rest of the country reeled from a stock market crash that only months before had unraveled the economy, the citizens of Mystic banded together to preserve the traditions and artifacts of their seafaring life.

Inspired perhaps by the holiday spirit of rebirth, Mystic residents Carl C. Cutler, Edward E. Bradley, and Charles K. Stillman chose Christmas Day to found The Marine Historical Association, which is known today as the Mystic Seaport Museum. The United States may have been speeding toward the Great Depression, but Cutler was determined to save a seaport that for centuries had been an enduring symbol of American strength and prosperity.

For nearly 300 years, the ocean was America's chief source of transpor-

tation and livelihood—as well as adventure. Even as other forms of travel and commerce eclipsed the sea's importance, it continued to support many sailors and seaside towns such as Mystic (which technically is not a town at all, but a fire district incorporating several neighboring communities).

Mystic's ties to the sea are rooted in the 1600s, when vessels were first launched from its shipyards. Although one of the smallest ports along the Atlantic seaboard, Mystic boasted a proud tradition of launching a greater tonnage of ships than any other port its size in America.

Fifty-six steamers were built in Mystic during the Civil War. The legendary *David Crockett,* a record-breaking clipper that made an unprecedented 25 voyages around Cape Horn to and from San Francisco, was launched from the Greenman family shipyard in the mid-1800s. Twenty additional clippers set sail

between 1851 and 1859. Many of the relics from America's shipbuilding glory days are preserved, thanks to the museum's founders.

The collections at Mystic were started in 1931 with a single vessel, a sandbagger by the name of *Annie.* Later that year, the Mystic Manufacturing Company—former site of the Greenman shipyard—was deeded to the association. From this meager start, the museum has grown into one of the most important maritime institutions in the world, covering 17 acres and 60 buildings.

More than boats have been preserved in Mystic, which is located along the Mystic River near its gateway to the Atlantic. An enchanting little seaside village—complete with restored homes, businesses, and actors portraying historical characters—Mystic reflects life in 19th-century America. Skilled artisans make maritime crafts ranging from

Above: *Students live aboard the fully rigged ship* Joseph Conrad *while they learn sailing basics on small boats. The Danish ship was built in 1882.*

Opposite: *Restored homes trimmed with greens line the village streets of the Coastal Life Area at Mystic Seaport Museum in Mystic, Connecticut. This view is seen through the rigging of the oyster sloop,* Nellie.

MYSTIC SEAPORT

wooden buckets to decorative shipcarvings. Handbills are printed daily at the old-time printer's shop. Visitors can also stroll through a bank, shipping office, grocery and hardware stores, chapel, schoolhouse, drugstore, nautical instrument store, and other homes and businesses that have been transported to the site.

Christmastime visitors to the seaport are invited to follow costumed guides on special yuletide tours aboard ships and through special exhibits depicting holiday scenes. Role players and the sounds of sea chanties add to the experience.

For nighttime tours, lantern light leads the way. Walking the dimly lit docks, one can nearly see the faces of the wind-whipped crewmen as they straggle ashore, and hear the fortunes jingling in the pockets of the prosper ous sea captains who lived throughout the village.

All of the buildings and shops at the museum are decorated for the holidays. Trims are either period appropriate or related to the sea. The Stone Store, for example, is dressed in greens and ribbons reminiscent of the Victorian era and displays a multitude of toys and small items for stockings at Christmas. Other buildings are bedecked in ropework and shell wreaths in keeping with Mystic's seafaring history.

More than 400 preserved vessels are housed indoors and out near the dock, making this collection of boats the largest in the United States and one of the largest in the world. Indoor exhibits include vintage photographs, maritime prints and paintings, ship models, and historical displays. During the holidays, Christmas trees are lashed to the tops of the masts of three of the largest ships. Smaller vessels are decked out in wreaths.

The museum's fleet includes both training ships and showpieces, many of which are the last remaining boats of their kind. The *Charles W. Morgan* (circa 1841), for example, is the only wooden whaling ship left in America, and the last commercial square-rigged American ship from the 19th century. A team of seamen provides sail-hoisting demonstrations upon this National Historic Landmark, training for weeks to be able to shimmy up the *Morgan's* mast.

As if this daring demonstration were not thrilling enough, the *Joseph Conrad* (circa 1882) invites participants in the museum's educational programs to actually try their hands at sailing a small boat. The *Joseph Conrad* is not the only hands-on exhibit at Mystic Seaport. The Children's Museum entices youngsters and their parents with its 19th-century toys and games, and a cache of reproduction clothing that children under age 7 can try on.

At the children's boat-building area, homemade vessels circle in the waters of an old-time clawfoot bathtub. When

the tub retires for the season, its roomy hull becomes a cozy spot for kids to read.

Other holiday festivities at the museum range from an afternoon concert by The Seaport Carolers, who lead visitors in favorite Christmas songs to "Kids After Christmas" week, a special week-long after-Christmas celebration for children, which features a variety of activities, including Plum Pudding voyages, games, crafts, and entertainment, just for youngsters.

The planetarium offers visitors yet another chance to step into the shoes of their seafaring ancestors. Gaze upon the starry nighttime sky—surrounded by the smell of saltwater and the gently lapping tide—and let yourself drift slowly and steadily out to sea.

At Christmastime, stargazing assumes added meaning, with visitors invited to attend the Planatarium's daily Star of Bethlehem programs.

Mystic's Christmas programs and activities run throughout December. For more information, write or call: Mystic Seaport Museum, 50 Greenmanville Ave., P.O. Box 6000, Mystic, CT 06355–0990; 203/572-0711.

Above: *During the mid-1800s, when wooden shipbuilding in America was at its peak, seaports such as Mystic had nearly all the business they could manage. Role players at this restored village reenact the days when Mystic was home to the prosperous whaling, merchant, and fishing captains who worked the seas.*

Left: *Shoppers at the Stone Store, one of the many re-created business in the Coastal Life Area, eye merchandise typical of the items stocked by stores in the 19th century.*

Opposite: *A young actress plays the role of one of the Greenman children decorating the tree for Christmas. During the 1800s, the family's shipyard built many important vessels at Mystic, including the legendary* David Crockett.

ACKNOWLEDGMENTS

PHOTOGRAPHS

Cover
   Hopkins Associates

Page 4
   Hopkins Associates

Page 5
   Perry Struse

Pages 6–7
   Perry Struse

Pages 8–15
   D. Randolph Foulds

Pages 16–21
   Hopkins Associates

Pages 22–25
   Rick Taylor

Pages 26–31
   Mike Moreland

Pages 32–37
   Jessie Walker

Page 38
   Timothy C. Fields

Pages 39–41
   Rick Taylor

Pages 42–49
   Maris/Semel

Pages 50–55
   Jessie Walker

Pages 74–79
   Jon Jensen

Page 80
   Hopkins Associates

Pages 81–87
   Jon Jensen

Page 88
   Hopkins Associates

Pages 89–94
   Jon Jensen

Page 95
   Hopkins Associates

Page 96
   Al Teufen

Pages 97–111
   Jon Jensen

Pages 114–115
   Tommy Miyasaki, De
   Gennaro Associates

Pages 116–117
   Michael Jensen

Pages 120–121
   Mike Dieter
   Photography, Inc.

Page 122
   Perry Struse

Page 123
   Michael Jensen

Pages 126–127
   Tommy Miyasaki, De
   Gennaro Associates

Pages 128–129
   Maselli/Sanders

Pages 130–131
   Tim Schultz

Pages 132–133
   Michael Jensen

Pages 134–135
   Mike Dieter
   Photography, Inc.

Pages 136–137
   Hopkins Associates

Pages 138–141
   Ernest Braun

Page 142
   Hopkins Associates

Page 143
   Left: Todd Tsukushi
   Bottom: Ernest Braun

Pages 144–153
   William Stites

Page 154
   Jon Miller, Hedrich-
   Blessing

Pages 158–161
   Maris/Semel

Pages 162–163
   Courtesy, Henry Ford
   Museum & Greenfield
   Village

Pages 164–165
   Courtesy, Colonial
   Williamsburg
   Foundation

Page 166
   Top: Courtesy, Colonial
   Williamsburg
   Foundation
   Bottom: Courtesy,
   Colonial Williamsburg
   Foundation. Reprinted
   from **Christmas
   Decorations from
   Williamsburg,**
   published by the
   Colonial Williamsburg
   Foundation.

Page 167
   Courtesy, Colonial
   Williamsburg
   Foundation. Reprinted
   from **Christmas
   Decorations from
   Williamsburg,**
   published by the
   Colonial Williamsburg
   Foundation.

Pages 168–171
   Courtesy, McGuire
   Studio and
   Conner Prairie

Pages 172–175
   Courtesy, Old Salem
   Inc.

Pages 176–179
   Courtesy, Henry Ford
   Museum & Greenfield
   Village

Page 180
   Courtesy, Ian M.G.
   Quimby

Pages 181–183
   Courtesy, Winterthur
   Museum

Pages 184–187
   Courtesy, Mystic
   Seaport Museum, Inc.

ARTWORK

COLLECTIBLES

REGIONAL EDITORS

INDEX

Page numbers in bold type refer to illustrations or illustrated text.